WHERE

MIRACLES

BEGIN!

*Jesus Christ said that you will
do greater things. It's time!*

LINDA ANDERSON

AuthorHouse™
1663 Liberty Drive
Bloomington, IN 47403
www.authorhouse.com
Phone: 1-800-839-8640

Published by AuthorHouse   02/12/2013

ISBN: 978-1-4817-1691-8 (sc)
ISBN: 978-1-4817-1690-1 (hc)
ISBN: 978-1-4817-1689-5 (e)

Library of Congress Control Number: 2013902848

"I say to you, he who believes in Me, the works that I do he will do also; and greater works than these he will do, because I go to My Father"
Jesus Christ (John 14:12-14).

Dedication:

To the Horizon and His Way Prayer Teams
who walk the purpose faithfully
ministering the love of Jesus.
You are indeed doing what
He said you would (John 14:12-14);
Your greater works
are evident!

And for Marla Dye, my faithful Ruth, who meant it when she said,
"Wherever you go, I will go . . ." (Ruth 1:16).

I also dedicate this book to my husband, Tom, who always
champions my dreams into reality. Your giving heart
is as big as the sky!

A special thanks goes to Pastor Jack Hayford for believing
in me and in this project.

CONTENTS

Introduction

MIRACLES BEGIN WITH PRAYER! No other vehicle affords us the possibility and pure joy of seeing people who were once held captive set free! In the name of Jesus, demons are cast out, healing occurs, oppression flees, heaviness lifts and all things are made new!

God has given me a vision. I believe that it is God-breathed and instigated. I can see it and feel the passion of it persistently. I see followers of Jesus Christ linked together by prayer around and encompassing the earth, connected like the links of a chain by prayer. A true prayer chain that wraps itself around the globe; not as bondage of chains, but as the strength of a mighty river!

God gives His dreams to people with the complete possibility of fulfillment. This book was written to help activate God's dream and to bring about His plan of victorious life for people!

As you read, try out the methods, exercises and proclamations given. You will be amazed because God is always so good to give a demonstration of His love (I Corinthians 2:4)! I hope that you will read with courage, experimentation and expectation.

To do great things for God you need the desire and the willingness - a desire to help people and the willingness to step forward. This book will help equip you to do what God has put in your heart.

If you are using this book for group training, I recommend that you close each teaching time by asking if there is anyone in the group who needs healing prayer. Practice the principles found in each chapter and you will experience God's power as He moves to bring healing. God loves to heal people and He will come and reveal Himself to you as you pray for one another. Stepping out like this will bring great reward.

As a companion to Where Miracles Begin, Prayer Team Training manuals are available for each individual in your group through His Way Ministries. These manuals teach how to form prayer teams in your church. At Horizon Christian Church we know that the formation of our prayer teams (Children's Prayer Team, as well as adult and youth teams) have been responsible for the rapid growth of the church.

The Prayer Team Training manual gives detailed instruction for every aspect of forming dynamic prayer teams. We also offer a Kid's Prayer Team Training Handbook.

Individual prayer, partnership prayer, marketplace prayer, and team prayer are the entire basis for cooperating with God. Prayer is where a miracle begins!

Dear reader, as you believe God for greater works through your life, may your faith be fully activated! The skills you will learn and apply will be life-giving as you go about your daily schedule. People who need help are all around you and you need the confidence, know-how and discernment to help them. These tools are found in this book!

Bless you as you believe God for miracles, in the name of Jesus!

Expecting Miracles,

Linda Anderson

PART ONE

MIRACLES BEGIN WHEN YOU ASK GOD

Speaking to groups outside of my own community of believers, I often tell about the miracles that we witness in Reno/Sparks, Nevada. Then I ask the listeners if they know why we see so many miracles. With this question the air becomes charged with expectation as individuals hold their breaths, waiting for the magic answer. The simplicity of the answer is in itself breath-taking: "WE ASK!"

"If you ask anything in My name, I will do it"
Jesus Christ (John 14:12-14).

Chapter 1

WHAT'S IN A NAME?

"When the multitudes saw [the miracles], they marveled and glorified God, who had given such power to men" (Matthew 9:8).

Do you have power that you don't know about? Does the church have authority to bless people that it isn't using?

One of the ways in which God propels us into the reality of His personal involvement in our lives is through unexplainable events. Without a supernatural occurrence which only God could perform, we might miss the joy of experience and the fulfillment of God's purposes through us. Miracles are not optional, they are essential to faith!

Like so many others, I was religious in my faith and devotion to God. Special encounters with His presence were occasional. I would some-times be aware of God's presence while attending a great church service or in a conference setting where passionate worship was present. Occasionally I would encounter someone who talked about God in a way that jarred me into a greater desire for Him.

Several years ago I had an astonishing experience while in the hospital that changed my life. My family lived in Oklahoma at the time I was hospitalized for a surgical procedure. Being close to the the center of Oral Roberts' ministry hub and university, it was common to see him on TV. As a renowned faith healer, Oral Roberts was a familiar name in Oklahoma. We knew of him, but as ministers in a conservative denomination, we didn't follow him.

There in the hospital, having just come through major surgery, I was in severe pain in my right arm. I kept telling my husband, Tom, that the pain of the incision was bearable, but that the pain in my arm was not. As I tried to rest, Tom turned on the TV and began to channel surf. Flipping through the channels, he rested for a moment on an Oral Roberts program — just long enough for me to hear the life-changing words, "There is someone with excruciating pain in their right arm listening right now. Be healed, in the name of Jesus!" Instantly ALL pain left my right arm and I was flooded with relief and astonishment. How could this happen with the sound of the words from a man on TV?! Something unexplainable had happened to me and I knew that it had to do with the name of Jesus! As I pondered the instant healing in my arm, I began to wonder what God was trying to tell me. And, I began to wonder if I could also have such authority to help people in my own ministry.

"If you ask anything in My name, I will do it" (John 14:14).

The pain in my arm was taken away and I was healed through the words of a person who had authority in the name of Jesus. There must surely be something exceedingly powerful about this name!

Throughout the Bible *names* have great significance to God. What a person is called (think about how many times you have been called by your own name) has an impact on his or her life.

One of the women in our church changed her name from "Rebel" to "Charity". When Charity was born, her parents named her "Rebel" (the meaning of rebel is *rebellion or against God*). Charity tells her story of how being called "Rebel" affected her life and caused her to become what she heard herself called —"rebellious". Later in life she accepted Jesus Christ as her Lord and Savior. As she grew to know God, she heard God speak to her heart about His desire for her to have a new name — "Charity", which means "God's love".

It was a challenging process for Charity to change her name legally as well as to help her family and friends adjust to her new name. But the result has been that Charity is reminded of who God says that she is whenever she is addressed by her new name!

In the Bible, we find accounts of where God changed the names of specific individuals. He changed Abram's name to "Abraham" by adding the "ah" that means *breath of God* (Genesis 17:5). The Lord did the same with Sarai as He changed her name to Sarah (Genesis 17:15).

When Saul was changed into a new man, he became Paul. God promised secret new names to others (Revelation 2:17), and was specific in what He wanted certain individuals called.

In Luke 1:13 we find the story of an angel being sent to give an unborn child a name. It was so important to God that John be called "John" that the angel, Gabriel, was sent to tell his dad this name.

Adam gave the animals names (Genesis 2:19); some people cried out to God for name-meaning changes (I Chronicles 4:10); the name of Jesus will eventually cause every person to bow down (Philippians 2:10)! The phrase, "the name of the Lord" is mentioned over one hundred times throughout the Bible.

Consider one more — God calls Himself "The Lord of Hosts" throughout Scripture (275 times — NKJV). These "hosts" are countless angels who serve God continually. He has innumerable – without number – servants and friends! (We will see later in this book how the ministry of angels is important to us as people.) God identifies Himself, more often than any other title, as the One who has countless angels who serve Him.

Jesus' Name: Unsurpassed In Power, Prestige and Possibilities

Names carry weight and have significance. Consider the effect when an American ambassador to a foreign country speaks in the name of the President of the United States. There is an authority that comes with this position and power that would not be avail-able to an ordinary tourist.

Think about what your response might be to having a police officer knock on your door and say, "Open up in the name of the law!" Most likely you would open the door because resisting could mean your arrest. There is power backing up that police officer!

How much more power is there when you are backed up by the name of Almighty God? Knowing the name that is above all names and being invited (requested by Jesus Himself) to use His name, is unsurpassed in privilege and power!

"At the name of Jesus every knee should bow, of those in heaven, and of those on earth, and of those under the earth, and that every tongue should confess that Jesus Christ is Lord, to the glory of God the Father" (Philippians 2:10-11).

When Jesus invites us to minister in His name He transfers divine authority to us. He gives us His power, prestige and possibilities. In the name of Jesus, anything good can happen!

The name of God is also a tremendous weapon against the powers of darkness. The authority in the name of Jesus Christ can drive demons out of an oppressed person. (Be cautious, though, that you do not use His name for personal gain or without proper respect. In Acts 19 we are told that some men tried to cast out a demon in Jesus' name, only to find that the demonic spirit knew they were phonies and called their bluff. The one demonized man beat up all the imposters and chased them out of the house. No one has the authority of Jesus unless Jesus Christ is truly their Lord!)

Your Authority In Jesus Christ Is Rooted In Your Relationship With Him

If you have asked God to forgive you of your sins, then this wonderful work of redemption has changed your destiny. Your name has been written in God's book in Heaven and you are now a child of God with all the benefits of being in His family.

Your relationship with God is legally based and not feelings based. For example, a newly married person may wake up the day after the wedding ceremony and not "feel married", but these feelings do not change the legal fact of their marriage. In the same way, no matter how you may feel on any given day, the place God has given you in His family is real. So is the power of God in your life. Your authority in God is based upon who you are in Him, through salvation, not on how you may or may not feel.

"For He has rescued us from the dominion of darkness and brought us into the kingdom of the Son He loves, in whom we have redemption, the forgiveness of sins" (Colossians 1:13-14).

Your salvation and adoption into God's family is a legally documented fact in the books of Heaven. According to the Word of God, when you received Jesus Christ as your Lord and Savior, you took on His name and you received His authority!

God Gave People Rule Over Planet Earth

As the people of God, we have authority that we may have not yet realized — and power that we probably are not using. God expects each of us to use the power He has entrusted to us to do great things on earth. You, as an inheritor of God's family name, have the great joy of helping people get freed, saved and healed, in the name of Jesus. The Bible provides us with many examples of people who accomplished amazing things because they knew their spiritual authority. Every example tells us the same underlying principle: Those who are raised up by God are backed up by God.

In the past God raised up Daniel, Esther, Nehemiah and others — just as He is raising you up! God gives us many examples in the Bible of people who did great things to inspire us. These people are not exceptions (the only ones who could do great things), they are examples; God wants you to know what you may also do. The same power He gave Daniel over a den full of lions is avail-able to you. In fact, the same power that raised Jesus from the dead, the power of the Holy Spirit, can reside in you too.

"But if the Spirit of Him who raised Jesus from the dead dwells in you, He who raised Christ from the dead will also give life to your mortal bodies through His Spirit who dwells in you" (Romans 8:11).

As people of the Kingdom, we need to know and operate in greater authority. Doing great things for God is thoroughly fulfilling for our own lives. Remember, though, God gives us authority for one specific purpose, and that is to fulfill His purposes on the earth.

7

What are God's purposes? Jesus said, ***"All authority has been given to Me in heaven and on earth. Go therefore and make disciples of all the nations"*** (Matthew 28:18-19).

It is our job to affect our culture and, even further, to bring the peoples of the nations to God; everyday people, like you and me, who desire more out of life and want to fulfill our destinies.

You may wonder why (since the name of Jesus has such authority and power) you often feel powerless to effect change. There may be a few things that you need to learn and even some that you may need to unlearn. God is at work right now, helping you reclaim the confidence that you may have lost. In the next chapter you will see how *renters in the house* messed up the plan. And how you can help set things straight.

Ask God:

Father, please give me an accurate picture of who You are and the authority that You have on earth. Wash off any false concepts that I have accumulated about You. Purify my heart and increase my confidence in You. Thank You that You will!

Questions

1. When have you spoken the name of Jesus and seen a change in a person or circumstance?

2. To whom has all authority in heaven and earth been given (Matthew 28:18)?

3. According to Luke 9:1 and 10:19, what did Jesus give His disciples authority over?

4. Are you a disciple of Jesus Christ? If so, then what has He given to you?

5. Read Mark 10:42-45. How will you exercise the authority that Jesus has given you?

For You to Pray:

Father, thank You for sending Your Son, Jesus Christ, to bring salvation to the whole world and especially to me! Please forgive me for the times that I have not honored and valued His name. Show me in deeper ways the great authority that is found in the name of Jesus! And please help me to walk in the strength of this authority as I help other people. Thank You that You will, in Jesus' name.

Chapter 2

You HAVE AUTHORITY (RENTERS IN THE HOUSE)

"When the multitudes saw [the miracles], they
marveled and glorified God, who had given
such power to men" (Matthew 9:8).

One morning, after reading news about a devastating earthquake, I was praying for grace and mercy for the people who lost loved ones. In prayer I heard the still small voice of God instruct, "Subdue the earth!" Surprised, I reached for the dictionary and found the meaning of the word "subdue"— *conquer, to tame, to reduce to mildness; to overcome; to captivate; to make less intense or less harsh; to soften; to destroy the force of* (Webster's Dictionary).

I remembered words that I had read in the Bible about *subduing the earth* but had never really paid attention to (Genesis 1:28). Could it be that it was God's expectation that I was to be part of subduing His earth? And what did this command really mean?

God said, "Let Us make man in Our image . . . let them have
dominion over . . . all the earth . . . and God said to them,
"Be fruitful and multiply; fill the earth and subdue it . . ."
(Genesis 1:26-28).

God has given you and me a job to do and it is no easy task! How do we tame the earth (quakes) and help bring calm to our planet?

In the days following the news of that devastating earthquake, geologists and prophets alike were predicting that other terrible earthquakes would take place. One of these quakes was projected to occur on the west coast of our nation within a month. Many Christians rose up in prayer, asking God to protect our nation and to show His mercy. As of this writing, a devastating earthquake has not occurred in our nation.

Did the many prayers of God's people subdue the earth? Was there an intercession by people that brought about the intervention of sovereign God into the affairs of our planet? We will only know when we see the whole picture someday in Heaven. But for now, we are called to bring peace through our lives and through our prayers of faith.

You might want to pause right now and ask God for the subduing of the earth under your own household. Ask God for rest and peace in your home, this nation, and the nations of the earth — and in your own soul!

Delegated Authority

"The heaven, even the heavens, are the LORD'S; But the earth He has given to the children of men" (Psalm 115:16).

From the beginning of time God delegated rule of planet earth to human people (Genesis 1:26-29, Psalm 115:16). God has never taken that rule away; people still have jurisdiction over planet earth.

Tragically, people capitulated and handed that rule over to Satan by sinning. All of us have contributed to the sin and evil problem on this earth through personal sin. We see the consequences of our own and other people's choices. Terrible things happen on this planet because each of us has chosen sin and selfishness at some point.

There has never been a single person born who did not sin — except Jesus! And although you may compare your small lies or bad attitudes to another person's "big sins" and justify yourself, God's Word states that we all have sinned and lost the authority to rule in full righteousness on our planet.

*"All have sinned and fall short
of the glory of God"* (Romans 3:23).

In the beginning, the devil didn't have any power on earth. He approached Adam and Eve in the Garden of Eden because he wanted control and power. The devil knew that God had given authority to Adam and Eve (and all human people yet to be born). The devil also knew that if he could get Adam and Eve to sin he would gain some power through them. The suggestion to eat the forbidden fruit was the devil's effort to get Adam and Eve to agree with him in opposition to God, thus empowering him. As we know, Adam and Eve sinned and gave power to the evil one; and down the line sin continued through each of us.

*"For since death came through a man, the resurrection of the dead
comes also through a Man"* (I Corinthians 15:20-22).

How could the rule over this planet, once given over to Satan, be redeemed? In view of the fact that God gave rule of the earth to people, a human person would have to take it back from the devil. But every human being has sinned and given place to the devil. Only a Person without sin could take back rule on this planet.

*"The ruler of this world is coming, and he
has Nothing in Me"* King Jesus (John 14:30).
"God is light and in Him is no darkness at all" (I John 1:5).

In the fullness of time, God sent His own Son, Jesus Christ, to earth as a human baby! Finally, there lived a Man who the devil could not work through! Satan had nothing in Jesus in which to stop full righteous rule on the earth (John 14:30)! Jesus took the authority, as a Man, that mankind had lost. When Jesus died on the cross, He stripped Satan of power (Colossians 2:15). Jesus Christ destroyed the works of the devil and still does as He reigns through us.

*"The reason the Son of God appeared was to destroy
the devil's work"* (I John 3:8).

Through the Cross and in the name of Jesus Christ, we now hold the power that was once lost to us. Through Jesus Christ we have the power to help loose other people from Satan's grip and set them free.

This life-giving power only comes through the Life-Giver, Jesus Christ. It is through His Holy Spirit inside of us that we accomplish His good works.

You might ask the question, "Since Jesus Christ took back rule of this planet, why is there still evil?" The answer is this: Jesus Christ bought back rule and authority at the Cross, but He hasn't taken full possession of earth yet.

Renters in the House

To give better understanding, let's use the example of a house that is leased out to renters. Let's say that you own a house but other people live in it. You are the owner, but you do not have possession; the renters who live there have control of your house. The house belongs to you, your name is on the deed, and you are responsible for the house. But, the people living in your house could still tear up your carpet, break your light fixtures and damage other parts of your house.

In the same way, even though the earth is the Lord's, He has "renters" messing with His property. It is our job to enforce His ownership and authority, and take care of His house!

> *"The earth belongs to God.*
> *Everything in it is His!"* (Psalm 24:1)

God has delegated power to you to rule for Him in your marketplace and neighborhood. God is the power behind your authority. The devil and his forces are obligated to recognize God's authority in you. The One who defeated Satan at the Cross is the One who lives inside of you. What will you do with the God of the universe inside of you?

God takes ownership THROUGH US, people who carry the Spirit of His sinless Son! We are brokers of His Kingdom — the very ones He works through to bring a release of His Kingdom on the earth! God is working through people to accomplish His purposes, and He wants to work through YOU!

> *"Behold, I give you the authority to trample on serpents and scorpions, and over all the power of the enemy, and nothing shall by any means hurt you"* King Jesus (Luke 10:19).

I heard this story from a preacher who told about standing on a street corner waiting for a bus. He said that a woman came out of an apartment house and her little dog ran out behind her. She said, "Honey, you're going to have to go back." The dog didn't pay any attention to her; he just wagged his tail and stood there. She said, "Now, dear, you can't go with me." The little dog wagged his tail and rubbed up against her. About that time, the bus arrived. The woman stomped her foot and yelled, "Get!" The dog tucked his tail between his legs and took off. The man telling the story said that he hollered out loud without even thinking, "That's the way you have to do with the devil sometimes!"

Jesus Christ said that we have authority over all the power of the devil. It is time to be willing, ready and able to use this authority confidently — armed with the truth of who we are in God as dearly loved children! We have authority over the devil in Jesus' name.

Love Relationship Is Not Satisfying Unless it is Chosen

It is evident that the choices we make do have an effect on the people in our spheres of influence. With the delegated rule that God has given to us as His children, we have responsibility to choose well. Remember that the devil wants to gain power through you and that God wants to subdue the earth through you. We are continually presented with choices of who will rule in the details of our individual lives.

Why would God give people the ability to choose good or evil when He knew what could happen to our world? It is evident as we read Scripture as well as through observation that God values *something* above the absence of evil in our world.

To God there is a gift that is more valuable than the absence of evil and that gift is free-will. As much as God hates evil, free-will is more valuable to Him than the absence of evil.

God gave you free-will because of the quality of relationship He wants to have with you. Love relationship is not satisfying unless it is chosen! In this very moment God has the power to demand trembling surrender from every human being on our planet. If He did this, not one of us would have a choice but to fall down before Him. But would this kind of surrender be what God desires?

Let's bring it down to how we, people made in the image of God, feel about love relationship. If a man (let's call him Joe) greatly desired to be married but could not find any woman who was interested in him, perhaps he would hatch a plan to take a bride by force. Joe could get into his car and go looking for his bride-to-be. Spotting a woman who looked like a good candidate, Joe might stop his car, grab the woman, throw her in his backseat and restrain her. Then, having found his fiancé, he could calmly drive to the justice of the peace (while the woman cried and screamed in his backseat), pay the justice to marry the two of them, and then drive off into the sunset to live happily ever after.

Of course there would be no happiness in this forced marriage and the kidnapped bride would be looking for a way to escape because relationship is never satisfying unless it is chosen. In the same way, our great God of love wants us to choose Him!

God does care about the evil taking place on the earth. In this account of the sorrow in God's heart before the Flood, we see that God cares deeply: ***"The LORD saw how great man's wickedness on the earth had become, and that every inclination of the thoughts of his heart was only evil all the time. The LORD was grieved that he had made man on the earth, and His heart was filled with pain"*** (Genesis 6:5, 6).

What would be the result of God ordering evil to cease on planet earth today? Free choice would be eliminated and people would be like robots. Love relationship would not be possible and the great love of the Father would go unsatisfied.

"The Father-Spirit turned toward the gates as they swung slowly open. His old accuser blinked into the distant splendor. 'Will You succeed this time in fashioning a lover who will remain a lover? Or is Your new creation destined to betray You?. . .The freedom that You always give becomes at last the very weapon that we level at Your heart.'" Calvin Miller, <u>A Requiem For Love, pages 11-13</u>

Giving God the love that comes from your own human free will I have chosen will delight His heart! It will also cause transformation in you, enabling you to bring about His activity and invasions into the affairs of earth! It is essential that a company of people arise in the midst of options and choose to love and serve God. Corporate obedience brings personal blessing and personal obedience brings corporate blessing.

Many People Remain In Bondage Because We Do Not Know The Power of Our Prayers

Recently, my husband, Tom, and I were on vacation in San Diego, California. As we visited one of our favorite churches on a Sunday morning, God opened my eyes to something amazing!

We were positioned just behind and across the aisle from two women. The one closest to the aisle was (from appearance and action) involved in an alternative lifestyle. During the pastor's convicting message, the woman kept falling asleep. Her head would fall forward, she would start awake and then quickly fall asleep again.

I began to silently cry out to God for her, interceding for her with a compassion that is only instigated by the Holy Spirit. I asked God to send her an angel to pinch her and keep her awake so that she could hear the message.

As I prayed (the pastor's message was over an hour, so I had plenty of time), at first there was no noticeable change, but I kept on praying with passion, asking God to send that prodding angel.

Suddenly, God opened my eyes to the unseen realm. As I looked, I saw a great angel having a conversation with a demon, right next to the sleeping woman! I could hear the demon arguing with the angel, insisting that the woman was his territory. As I watched, the angel turned abruptly and pointed at me! Needless to say, this really scared me! I felt this angel's action all the way through my body. Simultaneously, I saw that I had something that was reflecting radiant light down and toward the angel. Light that seemed to be somehow empowering the angel! Light was coming down from Heaven, reflecting off of me and empowering the spirit warrior!

I then saw the demon look from the angel, over at me, and then back at the angel. As it did, reluctantly the demon shrugged its shoulders and shuffled away. The opening to the unseen faded.

I sat in utter amazement, tears running down my face. With awe-struck wonder, I saw the woman for whom I had battled, awake and listening to the remaining part of the pastor's message — the part where he gave opportunity to receive Christ!

Our prayers have effect because we have positions of authority in the name of Jesus! When we pray, God dispatches angels to assist His work; when we pray, darkness has to submit to God; when we pray, good things happen! May you receive revelation from the Holy Spirit of this truth!

> **"Then Jesus said, 'All authority in heaven and on earth has been given to Me'"** (Matthew 28:18).

Step Out

The only way to find out what can happen through you is to step out in faith. Remember that your authority in Jesus Christ is based upon a legal agreement in Heaven, not on how you feel. (I tell the students in our ministry school, "If you are afraid to step out, step out afraid!")

As you step out in faith, arm yourself with God's compassion first. The fact that you are drawn to care about someone's need means that God is at work. If you care, you can be sure He is caring! And since God is caring, something good can happen!

Next, decide that if you pray for someone and you don't clearly see a healing, that you will not let that stop you from praying for more people. I often tell myself, *"If I pray for 100 people and not even one of them seems to be healed, I am going to pray for 100 more. Eventually, someone will get healed"* in the name of Jesus!

Ask God:

Father, please forgive me for my part in adding to the sin and selfishness on this earth. Help me to become a channel of Your love and goodness to people around me. Give me revelation of the truth of the authority you have delegated to me. I choose to serve You and to love You with all my heart!

Questions

1. What does the command of God, given to people, "subdue the earth" mean to you?

2. Why does the presence of evil continue on our planet when Jesus Christ has been given all authority over evil?

3. What is your part in bringing God's Kingdom rule into your sphere of influence?

4. How can you help the people around you get free of bondages?

Chapter 3

TURN AND LOOK (WHY WE GET BORED)

Divine Adventures Await People Who Keep Their Ears Open and Their Hearts Obedient.

Many people feel locked into a routine of the same day-to-day humdrum existence. I hear from individuals who say that their work is boring and life lacks excitement and sparkle. Maybe you have felt bored with your day-to-day life.

I used to wonder when the *great things* would kick in; that magic moment when I would begin to fully live every moment, from that time on, in the power of God. I kept waiting.

Occasionally, I would experience a God-encounter that would rev me up and keep me energized for days. But, for some reason, I didn't correlate the aliveness with the catalyst. I would soon settle back down, become bored and annoyed by the lack of adventure in my life, and wonder again when the aliveness would come and last *forever*.

In seeking God about my quandary, I found this question in the Bible, **"Why do you stand gazing up into heaven? This same Jesus, who was taken up from you into heaven, will so come in like manner as you saw Him go into heaven"** (Acts 1:11).

The essence of the question hit me, "What are you waiting for? Are you staring off into space? Do you expect to have your instructions written in the sky? It's time to get going . . . by the power of the Holy Spirit!"

Earlier in Acts (1:8), the Lord gave His disciples (and us) a job description. We are to be filled with power through His Spirit, and then be witnesses for Him. No more waiting for Him to do the job for us while staring into the sky and wishing. It is time to roll up our sleeves and get out there; out into the adventure of doing the *greater works* that Jesus intends for us to do.

This was the answer! Suddenly, it was clear to me that I had forgotten to begin my day by asking God to set up a divine encounter. On the days that I went looking for someone in need of healing, salvation or deliverance, I felt the grand adventure of life. On the days and then weeks when I forgot, I felt sluggish and ineffective.

Do you feel scared or unready to enter into the arena of being on the daily lookout for someone to minister to? Maybe you feel that you are not a bold person. Me neither. ALL my boldness comes from Holy Spirit power. Anyone can have this power — it just takes willingness and asking God. You can begin asking God as simply as this: "Lord, help me to become a *there you are* person instead of a *here I am* person!"

There You Are!

When my son and daughter were children, before going out the door each morning to school, I would remind them to be a "there you are" person. They knew what this meant (and do now, in each of their successful adult careers). I instilled into them the principle of walking into a room, forgetting about themselves and looking around to see who needed to be blessed and encouraged. With body language and words, they needed to say, *"There you are, you are important"* (as opposed to *"Here I am, make me feel good"*).

In the same way, you can be bold by remembering that other people need your help. You have something to give them; you have Jesus!

The Apostle Paul reminds us of the boldness and confidence we have at our disposal through faith in Jesus Christ. We have a job to do as we display the wisdom of God to principalities and powers in heavenly places.

"Grace was given, that [we] should preach among the Gentiles the unsearchable riches of Christ, and to make all see what is the fellowship of the mystery, which from the beginning of the ages has been hidden in God who created all things through Jesus Christ; to the intent that now the manifold wisdom of God might be made known by the church to the principalities and powers in the heavenly places, according to the eternal purpose which He accomplished in Christ Jesus our Lord, in whom we have boldness and access with confidence through faith in Him" (Ephesians 3:8-12).

We teach the students who attend our ministry school to ask God what He wants to do — and then to listen. The willingness to do what God wants us to do will attract His voice to speak to us.

Our students often go out in groups, looking for an opportunity to minister to people in the marketplace. When they have an encounter with someone who receives healing or salvation, the students come back into the classroom with unbridled excitement! They can barely keep their feet on the floor as what they experienced makes them feel as though they could *fly*. There is no boredom in these students. They may go out to minister like scared kids, but they come back as lion-hearted giants!

Deliverance in a Parking Lot

Recently, one of our ministry students had an unusual incident happen at her work place. As you read this story, notice the steps that brought deliverance to a girl named Ann*. In most cases the process of casting out demons is basically the same. May this story help to alleviate any fear you have had of not knowing what to do, or feelings of inadequacy in regard to helping with deliverance.

Ministry student, Elyssa Wood, works at *His Word Christian Bookstore* in our city and was the only employee on duty one evening when a distraught man and woman came in. The couple's troubled story began to unfold as they poured out their desperate need for help to Elyssa.

The woman told about how their "demon-possessed" (her words) daughter was in their car, outside in the store's parking lot. The family had been driving around trying to find some help. They asked Elyssa to please deliver their daughter from the evil spirits.

*Name Changed

Being the only employee on duty that night, Elyssa could not leave the store to go outside and to help the young woman. As Elyssa prayed, asking God for help, she discerned that she should call a man who serves on our prayer team and enlist help. Without delay, Elyssa made the phone call and connected with Todd Prinz. Todd was at church set-up along with a number of other individuals who serve on Prayer Team at Horizon Christian Church.

As Elyssa quickly explained the need, Todd moved immediately to mobilize a prayer team, letting her know that help would be there in less than 15 minutes. Elyssa quickly relayed this information to the upset parents who expressed amazement and gratitude that help was on the way.

Arriving just a few minutes later, the prayer team (Todd, Darlene, Tara, and Kristen) pulled up beside the only car in the store parking lot. Looking into the car, they saw the young teenager flailing about and kicking.

Armed with compassion and Holy Spirit boldness, the team assessed the situation while collecting information from the distraught parents.

(There is usually a little bit of nervousness that will try to come in at this point, no matter how many times an individual may have ministered deliverance before. The team God had assembled was not exempt from these feelings but each individual knew that it was time to overcome fear and take action.)

Tara began to speak the words, "Jesus Christ has all authority through the Cross and His shed blood." Kristen opened her Bible and began to read chapters four and five of Revelation out loud (see Strength Through the Book of Revelation at the end of this chapter). Todd began commanding the enemy to be silent, in the name of Jesus, and Darlene walked around the car proclaiming, "Jesus Christ is Lord!"

Prompted by the Holy Spirit, Darlene opened the door of the car. When she did, Ann went limp for a moment and then as Darlene took hold of the girl's arms, the demon began to fight. The others on the team immediately came to help and had a tough time keeping the demon from bringing harm as it fought for control. More proclamations of the authority of Jesus Christ were made; the demon was commanded to halt, and eventually Ann was able to cooperate with the deliverance team (although she was unable to speak).

The team bound a spirit of fear and the inability to speak, declaring the power of the Cross of Jesus Christ (demons are disarmed at the Cross according to Colossians 2:15). Darlene commanded the girl's tongue and vocal chords to be loosed by the power of Jesus Christ. As Ann's voice was freed, she was able to communicate with the team. By listening to the things that Ann said, clues were heard that indicated where the demons had place in Ann (see chapter 11, "Keys in Your Hand" for further insight).

Armed with boldness, there ensued a time of commanding the tormenting demons to leave Ann. Eventually she came into a place of release and healing!

After evident freedom came to Ann, she cried and hugged her family, telling them how sorry she was. As Ann asked forgiveness, Darlene instructed the family to say "I forgive you" in response. Darlene explained to them about the importance of the action of speaking forgiveness.

The relieved and amazed family began to ask the prayer team ministers some questions about what would happen next. They were assured that the demons were now gone and to not give place to fear. The family members were instructed to go home and read chapters four and five of Revelation out loud through their house and to walk in the truth of their authority in Jesus Christ. They were also instructed to invite the Holy Spirit to fill their home, hearts and minds, and to worship God. They were also encouraged to go to church and gain support and strength for their lives.

Following this instruction, Ann's mom told the story of how they had ended up at the bookstore that night in the first place. Earlier in the evening, as Ann began to manifest, thrashing violently and incoherently in their home, they didn't know what to do. In their desperation they decided to get in their car and drive somewhere — anywhere, to look for help. As they drove aimlessly along random streets, they felt like God was impressing on them to turn into a certain parking lot and look for a phone book so they could find a church location. As they pulled into the parking lot, they looked up and saw the sign for *His Word Christian Bookstore*, where Elyssa worked. Immediately, they parked the car, ran in and asked for help. The Lord led them to the right place! What an amazing story of how God orchestrates help for people! The series of God-orchestrated actions resulted in Ann's deliverance.

The next Sunday Ann's entire family showed up at Horizon Christian Church. When the individuals who were part of the team who had helped them heard that Ann and her family were in church, there was great excitement! The buzz spread throughout the church as the joy of the testimony multiplied and filled the house. There is nothing that lights up a life and a church like being part of a miracle!

A divine encounter, inspired by the Master Orchestrator, awaits each of us as we are willing. How the Lord loves people, and how He longs to use our lives to set others free!

Destiny Restored!

I long to see the people of God energized and His world evangelized! How about you? Are you ready for divine adventures?

Through Ann's story, you read the steps for bringing deliverance to a person who is oppressed by demons. As you have read, hopefully you have understood that the process is not too complicated. Actual experience in a deliverance session will take away the fear of the unknown and arm you with courage to help those who are bound. You just have to be willing to help others and to find experienced people who you can accompany on a divine adventure!

God will orchestrate His great plan if you are willing to partner with Him. That night at the Christian bookstore parking lot, all the team did was follow direction from the Holy Spirit because they were willing.

One of our ministry interns, Kristen Velasquez, shared what she wrote in her journal after the encounter at the bookstore: *"This just proves that God's timing is absolutely perfect and His plan is flawless. From the time the family left their house, to the parking lot they turned into, to the person working at the bookstore that night, to the day and time of the week, everything that happened was divinely orchestrated by God. The deliverance of that precious girl was contingent upon a series of choices to be obedient to the Holy Spirit's promptings. That night a girl's destiny was restored!"*

Turn and Look!

The Bible is full of real examples of times in which God opened doors of opportunity for people to partner with Him. Many of the adventure stories are not big lightning-bolt encounters. Like Moses, the only thing you may have to do is be ready to turn and look.

Moses may have been totally bored on a day when all *normal* life for him ended. Out tending his sheep on an ordinary day something extraordinary happened. But Moses had to look. The Bible states that God spoke to Moses when He saw that Moses paid attention, turned aside from his routine, and looked!

"The Angel of the LORD appeared to [Moses] in a flame of fire from the midst of a bush. <u>So he looked</u>, and behold, the bush was burning with fire, but the bush was not consumed. Then Moses said, '<u>I will now turn aside and see</u> this great sight, why the bush does not burn.' So when the <u>LORD saw that he turned aside to look</u>, God called to him . . ." (Exodus 3:1-4).

Moses looked! We can so busily move through our days that we forget that something extraordinary could happen. When Moses looked, it was then that God spoke to him.

Moses' destiny changed forever in one afternoon when he turned and paid attention to the shift God wanted to bring in his life.

On The Job Training

As we shift into paying close attention to what God is doing, we find that He is very interested in people. He desires to help people and He just needs someone to facilitate His miracles.

One day the disciples came to Jesus and told Him that a crowd of people needed food. The multitude had followed Jesus into a desolate place and now they were hungry. Jesus' answer to the disciples was, *"You give them something to eat"* (Mark 6:37). And they did!

Jesus trained His disciples to do the miraculous right on the spot and at the point of need. No doubt the disciples felt unqualified and inadequate — until they gave it a try and it worked!

Jesus' method of doing miracles through you is to train you on the job. Your boldness and confidence will come through your time in seeking to know Jesus Christ and finding out what He wants done.

"When they saw the boldness of Peter and John, and perceived that they were uneducated and untrained men, they marveled. And they realized that they had been with Jesus" (Acts 4:13).

The most valuable thing that each of us possesses is our time. What we give our time to will ultimately define who we are. To be an effective minister will require that you make time alone with God a priority. Confidence and boldness flow from a heart that hears God and loves God. No one else can do this part for you. What you give your time to will ultimately define who you are.

Jesus found some people who were willing to give their time to being with Him. These were the ones who Jesus sent out to do the work of the ministry.

The Lord sent twelve men out to do a job that they would learn how to do while they were doing it. Jesus didn't wait until the disciples were experienced, He sent each person out into ministry at a point that others may have considered too soon.

Most of us believe that people need to be fully prepared prior to doing ministry. We think that this will ensure that nothing will happen that will mess up reputations or harm our families. But, the way that we mature in life is through serving in ministry!

Consider the biblical account following the disciple's return from their healing, deliverance and preaching campaigns. They were just barely back with Jesus when they began to display their immaturity. James and John were feeling powerful and prideful after their great exploits on the mission field and were ready to call down fire on anyone who did not receive Jesus.

His disciples James and John . . . said, 'Lord, do You want us to command fire to come down from heaven and consume them, just as Elijah did?' But [Jesus] turned and rebuked them, and said, 'You do not know what manner of spirit you are of'" (Luke 9:54-55).

Serving God will help to reveal what is in your heart. When the disciples returned with such pride about the things that they had accomplished, you might think that Jesus would tell them to get rid of the pride before He sent them out again. But instead, He was so excited about what happened with the twelve that He immediately sent out 70 others!

"After these things the Lord appointed seventy others
also, and sent them two by two before His face into every
city and place where He Himself was about to go. Then
He said to them, "The harvest truly is great, but the
laborers are few; therefore pray the Lord of the harvest
to send out laborers into His harvest" (Luke 10:1-2).

In most church culture, if a person admits that he or she has problems or issues, it is a disqualifier for ministry. Not with Jesus! The culture of the Kingdom does not give room to cover, conceal and hide ourselves. In fact, the more honest we become, the more open we are with God to receive revelation, insight, authority and power (James 5:16).

Are you willing to be so bold that you put yourself *out there*? You may want to be perfect prior to ministry. But the way that you mature is by serving in ministry!

While the Temple Was in Chaos, the Miracles Began

Consider what happened in Jerusalem on a day when Jesus came to town and went straight into the temple (Matthew 21:1-16). Ordinary people were buying and selling the things that they needed to offer sacrifices to God. Temple business as usual — until the Son of God came in and began to make a mess. Turning over tables and scattering money, baskets and birds everywhere, the temple was in an uproar!

Jesus entered the temple and cast out . . . and overturned . . . and
He said to them, "It is written, MY HOUSE SHALL BE CALLED A
HOUSE OF PRAYER" (Matthew 21:12-13).

This account in Matthew 21 gives us a very important picture of how miracles can flow even when things are not perfect — in fact, far from perfect!

Jesus made a mess of the temple, and while it was in chaos, people slipped in who were normally prohibited from entering. Lame and blind people who were considered "unclean" could not enter the temple on a normal day; but they got in and were healed on the day Jesus walked in and changed everything.

"Then the blind and the lame came to Him in the temple,
and He healed them" (Matthew 21:14).

Do you see the analogy? When you ask Jesus Christ to forgive your sins and come into your life, you become a temple for God (I Corinthians 6:19). But your temple needs cleaning out. There are habits, attitudes and issues that need to be dealt with by God. Jesus comes into your life and He begins to change you and overturn the way that you do things. You look a mess and you may very well feel like a mess. But, note this very encouraging and good thing: while your temple is still a mess, you can establish it as a house of prayer, and then the power will come for miracles! You don't have to have it "all together" to be a house for God!

Minister While You Are In Process of Becoming Who You Will Be

The Bible teaches that *"you are God's building"* (I Corinthians 3:9). *"Do you not know that your body is the temple of the Holy Spirit who is in you . . . and you are not your own?"* (I Corinthians 6:19). *"For you are the temple of the living God"* (II Corinthians 6:16).

The miracles that God wants to do through you will come as you make your life a life of prayer, allowing God to turn over your old ways of doing things, and going ahead with serving God while you are in process of becoming who you will be.

Even the Apostle Paul said, *"Christ Jesus came into the world to save sinners, of whom I am chief"* (I Timothy 1:15).

Become Bold in Your Witness

Praying for boldness is like praying for patience. You will be given opportunities to test out your courage and gain experience. God will call you to a course, and in the midst of that course there will be anxiety, feelings of inadequacy and fear. Don't let fear stop you from being bold for God — if you are afraid to step out, do it anyway — do it afraid!

God is ready to pour the weight of His worth into your life! The weight of God's worth brings self-worth. So, invite Him to pour into you. Find people who are bold for Jesus and ask them to pray for you.

Find Your Voice

Many people are afraid of their own voice — afraid to pray out loud, afraid to even say, "Praise the Lord" when something good happens. Practice saying these things out loud when you are alone with God and get comfortable. Soon you will find yourself witnessing and honoring God *out there*!

"Being confident . . . He who has begun a good work in you will complete it" (Philippians 1:6).

Invite the Holy Spirit to give you a boldness that will translate into a life of miracles through you!

David's Mighty Men

Before we moved to Reno/Sparks, Nevada to plant a new church, the Holy Spirit began to give us mandates for the church. One of the directives God gave was for us to look at the potential of people and not evaluate their current state. The Lord showed us that He would bring us people, but we might not recognize them if we weren't looking with His eyes.

The Lord encouraged us to look for and enlist people like David's mighty men: *"Everyone who was in distress, everyone who was in debt, and everyone who was discontented gathered to [David]. So he became captain over them"* (I Samuel 22:1-2). David's Mighty Men became warriors and amazing leaders (II Samuel 23:8).

As we have looked at each individual's potential, we have raised up and trained strong leaders who had no idea that God could use them so powerfully!

Strength Through the Reading of Revelation

Another way in which you can gain strength and become free from fear is to listen to the book of Revelation. God gave an amazing promise to those who will listen to and read the incredible book of the Bible, Revelation! In Revelation 1:3, He said, *"Blessed is he who reads and those who hear the words of this prophecy"*. Do you want to be blessed? This promised blessing is available to you!

Recently, as I was speaking to a group of leaders about prayer, I encouraged them to listen daily to the Book of Revelation on CD or MP3, knowing it would bring blessing and strength to their lives. Later I asked the Lord to reveal to me the reason why the Book of Revelation brings such blessing. The Holy Spirit gave me the following insight:

Meditating on Revelation brings blessing because of a lie that needs to be forged out of every person. Satan tries to convince every individual (in one way or another) that he will win — that evil will win. Every person has seen temporary evil "win" in their life or the lives of others and have been frightened by it. This secret fear is so deep that it may be completely hidden from a person, coming out only in dreams or other subconscious ways.

The Book of Revelation is all about the True Champion, Jesus Christ! He is proclaimed the Victor, the Champion, and the Ultimate-For-All-Time Winner! Listening to this truth in the Book of Revelation mines out fear and the lie that says that evil might win. It pours light and truth into the soul and eradicates the lies. No wonder it brings blessing! To increase boldness, confidence and strength, feast on the Revelation of Jesus Christ! You will be fully nourished by God!

As you are strengthened in faith, there will be no more of the hum-drum life you once knew. Life is an adventure and the hunt is on. Turn and look; there is something God wants you to see right now!

Steps in Preparation for a Divine Adventure

1. Pray for personal revival; ask God to cleanse you and bring you into alignment with His love (Acts 3:19).

2. Ask God to give you a great desire to see the lost saved and make you a vessel so full of His Holy Spirit that love will over-flow through you like a river (John 7:38).

3. Use your mouth to declare that no power or principality will prevail against you or your church and that your entire community will be saved (Matthew 16:18-19)!

4. Pray for boldness for yourself and for your brothers and sisters in the Lord!

5. Pray for divine encounters — THIS WEEK — for yourself and those around you (II Timothy 4:2-5).

6. Make a list of people who you want to follow around and learn from.

For You to Pray:

Father, I want to be brave enough to step out into divine adventures for You. I need my eyes opened to what You are doing so that I can discern where You are working. Please open my eyes to the things of Your Spirit! Show me the real things that are taking place and help me to look deeper and not just skim the surface. Give me a divine encounter today! I am willing to serve in any capacity You want me to. In Jesus' name, amen.

Chapter 4

OBEDIENCE BRINGS BLESSING

"If you love Me, keep My commandments"
King Jesus (John 14:15).

When Tom and I were planning our wedding (four decades ago), it was common for the vows spoken during the ceremony to include the word obey. A typical line in a bride's vows to her groom was, "I will love, honor and *obey.*"

Obey was not a word that I wanted in my vows and so I took it out. Having to obey was for kids living at home with parents and I was about to come out from under having to obey anyone anymore! Or so I thought.

It was years later, as I was preparing to teach others on the subject of obedience to God that the Holy Spirit brought up my wedding vows attitude. He reminded me of what I had done when I took the word *obey* out and showed me the rebellion in my heart. It wasn't so much that God wanted me to say "obey" as He wanted me to love enough to be obedient!

When the Lord showed me my wrong attitude I repented. As I repented, a new freedom came into me that I had not experienced before. Seemingly such a small thing and yet it had a harbor in my soul that affected certain aspects of my life. Whereas I had often felt irritated when asked to do some act of service, after the Lord cleansed me, I noticed a true joy in serving. I found a freedom that surprised me and it came through asking the Lord to show me the hidden little things that were diminishing my joy and potential.

Everyone has hidden things inside of themselves that only the Holy Spirit can reveal and heal. This is one of the great benefits of being a child of God! We can gain greater freedom in daily life as we invite the Holy Spirit to help us.

Little Things

Recently we had a family breakfast with French toast, butter, and syrup. After we enjoyed the delicious food we all began to clean up. I went to get a Ziploc bag to put the remainder of the butter in, but before I could put it in the bag, someone else stuck the saucer — with the uncovered butter — in the refrigerator. I asked where the butter was and then saw how it had been put away.

I asked the family member if she remembered that we always wrap butter because it absorbs refrigerator odors. She sheepishly replied that she did remember. Then I laughingly asked if she felt a little nudge from her conscience when she put it away incorrectly. She admitted that she did feel a twinge but dismissed it. Then I asked the question, "Do you know that the still small voice of God speaks to you in your conscience? If you ignore or discount this voice, you will struggle with hearing the voice of God in larger matters." Stunned silence followed as the revelation sunk in. Ignoring the conscience can inoculate you (make you immune and resistant to) hearing the inside Voice in bigger matters!

How Can Such a Small Thing Affect Your Ability to Hear God's Voice?

When I was growing up my family lived in a rural neighborhood where our next door neighbor had chickens. When we first moved in and heard the roosters crowing early in the morning we were bothered. But after several weeks no one in my family was awakened by crowing any longer. We had all gotten used to the roosters crowing and didn't hear them anymore. But when we had overnight guests, they would complain about the noisy crowing early in the morning. They could hear what my family no longer noticed!

If we continue to ignore something, pretty soon we won't hear it at all. If we have ignored God's quiet voice in small things, we may not be able to perceive His voice when we need to hear Him in bigger things.

The first step toward reinstating your ability to hear God is to ask Him to speak to you in everyday ways, and tell Him that you will obey Him.

Deciding to Listen to the Quiet Voice of God Changed My Life!

When I was in my thirties I was living the *good Christian life,* serving in the church, and trying to do *everything* right. But there was something missing and I knew it. I didn't have the *"joy unspeakable and full of glory"* that we sang about in church. I had a yearning too deep to explain and knew that I needed something more.

I became desperate for a closer relationship with God and in this desperation I became willing to do anything that would help me. One night I made a promise to God. I told Him that I would obey anything that He asked me to do, even if I wasn't absolutely certain that it was Him asking. If what I thought God might be saying to me lined up with the Bible, I would do it.

Immediately following this radical promise to God, challenging things began to happen. One of the first tests came on a Wednesday night. I was browning hamburger at the kitchen stove in preparation for the family dinner before going to the evening prayer meeting at church. As I stood at the stove, I looked out the window and saw one of my neighbors washing off her driveway with a water hose. Seemingly out of the blue I thought that I might have heard a very quiet voice ask me to go out and talk with her. And just as quickly, my mind began to rationalize why this couldn't be God speaking. Surely He knew that I was already running late in getting dinner ready for my family before church. Anyway, my neighbor was busy and might go in before I could get out there. And what was I supposed to say to her anyway?

But I had promised God that I would obey even if I wasn't sure it was Him who was speaking to me.

Grumpily, I turned off the heat and set the pan aside. I grabbed my shoes and went out the front door. With no time to spare, I approached my neighbor with a simple "hi". She didn't even look up as she said a busy "hello" and kept washing her driveway. I tried again, "How are you?" "Fine." "Nice weather." Silence.

I hovered a couple more minutes and then in embarrassment I went back inside and to the kitchen, all the while thinking, "I can't hear God." And sure enough, we were late to church.

It was the very next day that another test came. As I was doing morning chores, the thought came into my mind, "Call and go see Fern Allen." (Fern was an older woman in our church — a woman of prayer and strong faith.) Again, my mind began to refute this idea, "Why should I call Fern? What would I say to her? I have too much to do today already."

Then I remembered my promise — I would obey God even if I wasn't sure it was Him speaking.

Going to the phone and finding Fern's number, I silently prayed that she wouldn't answer. Fern answered on the second ring. "Hi Fern, this is Linda Anderson. I am wondering if I could come over some time and visit with you." Without hesitating, Fern replied that I should come over right away. Oh great.

Walking up to Fern's front door, I rehearsed what I would say to her, "I am just coming by for a minute to see how you are doing." But before I could even knock, Fern threw the door open wide and pulled me inside. It seemed that I was not the one in control of this meeting. Drawing me over to the couch, she pressed me down onto the floor as she explained that she wanted to pray for me.

Putting her hands on my back, Fern began to cry out to God to bless me and fill me with His Spirit! With surprised embarrassment I suddenly realized that I wasn't the only one who knew that I desperately needed God to do something in me. This encounter at Fern's house was humbling and bewildering. I walked out her door an hour later wondering if anything had changed in me and hoping that somehow it had. Unusual and humbling things like the encounter at Fern's house were obviously on God's heart. It was the next week, while attending a pastor's conference with all male pastors that I bumped into the next difficult challenge.

Standing shoulder to shoulder in worship with the group, I already felt out of place as a woman pastor. I wanted to be as unobtrusive as possible and was totally caught off guard when I thought I heard the quiet voice of God ask me to bow down on my knees in worship. Now

He had gone too far. I argued that there was no room; I complained that surely He knew that I was wearing a skirt; I told Him that my husband would not appreciate this action. Silence. And I remembered again my promise — I would obey God even if I wasn't sure it was Him speaking.

With tears of mortification running down my face, I sunk to my knees in obedience to my promise. And instead of worshipping with my heart and not just with my body, I silently begged for reprieve and hoped that I might rise. Eventually the song ended and I slowly got to my feet. My only consolation was that my husband's eyes were closed and he had not even noticed my action.

The tests were getting harder and in fact, were just about to become unbearable. It was the next Sunday in church that a deeper humbling was about to unfold. My pastor husband had just given an excellent salvation message and was opening the altars for seekers to come forward and be saved. The music minister was leading the congregation in the hymn, "Just As I Am" and I was praying for seekers to be brave and move out of their pews and to the altars when I thought I heard God say, "Go to the altar." My first thought was "How ridiculous, I am already saved; I am the pastor's wife!" My second thought was, "Oh no, not this, Lord, You have got to be kidding!" I began to pray harder for seekers to go to the altar. If someone would just move toward the altar, I could fulfill my promise to obey God's voice by going forward to pray for someone else. But no one was moving toward the altar! I heard my husband say, "I know there is someone God is waiting for. Won't you come? We will wait as we sing another verse."

Mortified and sobbing with humiliation, I stepped out to keep my promise to God. I was desperate for an encounter with Him and would move out to obey His voice, even if I wasn't sure it was Him. (I was pretty certain that the devil wasn't trying to get me to go to the altar and I knew the idea had certainly not come from my own heart.)

Kneeling down, I heard my husband say, "One person has come. Let us surround her with prayer." I could feel people gathering around me, laying their hands on me and praying, "Hold on, Linda!" "Let go, Linda." "Give it up, Linda." "Don't give up, Linda." If I had not been crying so hard, I would have laughed! Those around me thought that God surely was doing a mighty work as the pastor's wife was sobbing so hard. And they were right. God was pulling pride and looking good in front of people out of me.

Weeks of God-orchestrated humbling events were the painful way of change for me. It became increasingly clear that I had much pride that stood in the way of the relationship I needed with God. The Master Orchestrator knew what He was doing and had initiated the way to bring me into what I truly needed and desired.

The Air Was Charged With Electricity and Light!

Following many weeks of trying to act on what I thought might be the voice of God, one night I had a magnificent Holy Spirit encounter! My husband and children were away for the evening and I had some extra time to spend in prayer. Still desperate for more, I knelt in prayer, asking God to do something in me that would change my life.

That night as I cried out to God again, I could feel something happening. The air around me seemed charged with light and electricity. I could feel the intense presence of God in the room and the feeling was glorious! It was as if a light from Heaven encircled me where I knelt and was pouring into me! Something new and wonderful was happening to me and I was filled with unspeakable joy! I could feel hot liquid love pouring into me and then pouring out from my own mouth to God.

I was crying, laughing and shaking all over. There was just nothing in my life to compare with what I felt. Every temporal thing seemed to melt away as I was saturated with God's presence and love! It was as if all of Heaven was opened to me and swallowed me up in joy!

I was so filled and transformed by the Holy Spirit that nothing else mattered. Even a couple of hours later when my family returned home, I was still overwhelmed with the intensity of God's presence. I tried to tell them but no words could describe what had happened to me.

The weeks and months following this experience were filled with joy and wonder. I would often wake my husband up in the night just to tell him how happy I was! Tom would pat my arm and tell me that I already told him and to go back to sleep. I could hardly sleep — my heart was so full of fire, love and joy!

This Will Not Be Taken From Her

At first I was afraid that I would lose the freshness and glory of this life-changing encounter. I begged God daily that He would not take the intensity of His presence from me.

Fear of losing my newfound joy drove me to seek God continually for more. One day He gave me the verse, ***"But one thing is needed, and Mary has chosen that good part, which will not be taken away from her"*** (Luke 10:42). Keeping this verse in my thoughts pushed out the fear as I believed that the good thing God did for me would not be taken away! Now, even after more than 20 years, the joy has not left me.

The mysterious part of what God did for me is that I did not even know that I was disobedient to Him. I thought that keeping certain rules (like the ones I was raised with in church) was all that was required and that I was a fine Christian. I didn't know that I was living my own way with a form of godliness. I just knew that I had no joy or power (II Timothy 3:5).

God is the Great Initiator!

There is no life in keeping rules because life is found in the voice of the Lord! Jesus said, ***"The words that I speak to you are spirit, and they are life"*** (John 6:63). When He speaks, we come alive!

Your desire to hear God and know the joy of His presence is initiated by Him. You didn't come up with the desire to live in glorious union and communion with Him — this is God's idea and He intends to fulfill this desire! You may think that you are waiting on God to do something wonderful in you, but maybe He is waiting on you. Even now He is calling your name and drawing you into a deeper encounter with Him. All you will have to give up is yourself. But who would hold onto living for themselves when they can live in the great expanse of God's love and glory?

You want to hear God. He wants you to agree to obey His voice in love before He speaks to you. This one thing will attract His voice — your willingness, desperation and agreement to obey. As we are obedient, God gives us more!

Kingdom Ways

In the culture of the Kingdom of God, using the gifts that God has already given us is what brings reward and increase. Jesus said, *"For to everyone who has, more will be given"* (Matthew 25:29). To receive more from God, I must be obedient with what He has given me already. If I only have the quiet voice of my conscience, I need to obey it in the little things If I steward in the little, the Lord will entrust me with more!

Think of the little boy who gave Jesus his lunch (John 6:1-13). Such a small lunch, but a possibility lunch! And because of this lunch, what did thousands of people eat? They had a nice fish and bread lunch! God can take even the little that you have and multiply it to feed many.

Jesus always multiplies what you have. What do YOU have for God to multiply?

Do you want *more* from God? The way to be given more is to be grateful for and use what He has already given you. What has He given you? How are you doing in being obedient with what you already have?

Personal Obedience Brings Corporate Blessing!

As we individually love God (as the little boy with the lunch did), an entire community of people gets fed and blessed. Imagine what would happen if many of us become obedient to God!

The Lord instructed Peter, *"If you love Me . . . feed My sheep"* (John 21:17). If you love God, you will obey His commands. If you love God, you will help to feed others.

You may feel that you have been short-changed and that God didn't give you what you need to feed others. Maybe it seems as though you don't have what others need. Or it could be that you feel disqualified to help others because of your past or present circumstances. All of these thoughts (and many more that seem so true) are common deceptions and temptations that the devil uses to hinder the work of God through people. If the devil can stop individuals from using their God-given gifts to help others, he can stop the blessing to the multitudes. It is imperative that you fight the devil's temptation!

God wants to help you right now. Are you willing?

Invite the Holy Spirit to Search You

Pause and ask God to show you if there are any lies which you have believed that limit your obedience to His will for your life. Welcome Him to search you and then quiet your heart to listen.

Ask the Holy Spirit to show you what the gifts are that He has given you to be used to bring blessing to others. Ask Him to raise up people who will recognize and affirm your gifts.

Tell the Lord that are you willing to obey Him in anything He asks.

Expect to be a little (or a lot) scared about telling God that you will do anything. Then decide that you will obey even if you have to do it afraid. He will strengthen you! And as you go, God will bless you and give you more than you could even hope for!

Questions

1. How can ignoring the little nudge of your conscience hinder you from hearing the great voice of God?

2. What one thing are you afraid God might ask you to do (if you agree to obey anything He asks)?

3. Have you had experiences with God in the past that seem to have faded away? What did Jesus tell Mary about her choices?

4. How can your personal obedience to God bring blessing to others?

For You to Pray:

"Search me, O God, and know my heart; try me, and know my anxieties; and see if there is any wicked way in me, and lead me in the way everlasting" (Psalm 139:23-24).

Chapter 5

TRAIN YOUR EARS TO HEAR

Jesus said, "The words that I speak to you are spirit,
and they are life" (John 6:63)

You were born and created to be with God, to move the heart of God, and to get answers to prayer. It is actually part of your personality and makeup to rejoice in and experience continual answers to prayer; to talk to God and to hear Him talk to you.

Jesus said that the words He speaks are spirit and they are life (John 6:63). When God speaks, everything changes! You may be thinking, "if only I could hear God." But take heart, the Bible states that you can!

If you have asked Jesus Christ into your life, you have already heard God's voice. We can only come to God through Jesus Christ if He has drawn us. He is the great Initiator! King Jesus said, *"I am the way, the truth, and the life. No one comes to the Father except through Me"* (John 14:6). *"Here I am! I stand at the door and knock. If anyone hears My voice and opens the door, I will come in"* (Revelation 3:20).

What Does God Want to Say to You?

People often communicate with one another for information. "Which restaurant do you want to go to?" "Where did you put my cell phone?" "I'm going to bed." But God usually communicates for relationship.

So many times I have come to the Lord in prayer hoping to get some information. "Which job should I take? Where is the money going to come from to take care of these problems? Should we buy that house?" Oftentimes, while I am asking questions, if I will become quiet enough, I can hear God answer, "Linda, I love you."

With the Lord, love is always first and primary. Even in the way He commands us to relate to Him, heart is always first on the list.

> ### *Jesus said, "You shall love the Lord your God with all your heart, with all your soul, and with all your mind"* (Matthew 22:37).

Throughout the Scripture, whenever the greatest command is stated, heart is always first on the list and top priority. The words that follow "heart" (soul, mind and strength) may vary and are interchangeable, but every single time the command is given, heart is on top. I believe that the sequence, the fact that God desires love from our hearts above all else, is as inspired as the words that are used. Everything about God points to the fact that He is love and wants our love in return.

What is heart-love? Think of a time when you experienced extravagant, unexplainable and unconditional love for another person. Maybe it was while holding your newborn baby; perhaps you watched a loved one receive a special award or honor and your heart swelled with joy beyond words; or the feeling of first love awakening with the one you would marry. Although these feelings cannot compare with the great love of God, these experiences hint at the undemanding freedom from time constraints, and purity of His love. God wants to walk with you in the cool of the day (Genesis 3:10), just to enjoy your company.

Training Your Ears

Many people miss the joy and comfort of being with God because they don't understand how He communicates. Yet, hearing God's voice is a basic privilege of every believer. The Lord said *"My sheep hear My voice, and I know them, and they follow Me"* (John 10:27).

We are the ones who make listening to God and hearing from Him complicated. If you really want to please and obey Him, God has promised that you can wait on Him and He will speak to you. *"You will seek Me and find Me, when you search for Me with all your heart"* (Jeremiah 29:13).

In my life I wanted to be able to hear God daily. I wasn't satisfied with the occasional experience of hearing Him. One-sided conversation in prayer felt boring to me. So, I set out to learn how to discern God's voice from all the other voices that contend for my attention.

Each day I spent time crying out to God that I might hear Him. I did this for almost four years before I finally had real breakthrough.

Along the way there were times when God spoke to me; I knew it, and things changed inside of me because I heard Him! One of those times was when I was ready to give up and run away from a difficult situation.

I had just arrived at a campground where I was to speak at a women's retreat. The campground was unexpectedly rustic and I was given a remote cabin in the woods. The man who showed me to my cabin explained that the door didn't lock and that he was sorry it had not been fixed. Feeling terribly uncomfortable and wondering how safe I would be alone that night, I thanked the man and watched him leave in his truck. I walked over to the bed to check and make sure there were sheets. Pulling back the covers, I was appalled to find a huge spider in the bed! That was it — I would let the retreat leaders know that I couldn't stay.

Pausing to ask God what He had to say about this retreat at which He had led me to speak, I heard very clearly, "Peace, be still, Linda."

Immediately and fully, peace flooded through my body and soul! Amazed and grateful, I found a broom to sweep the spider from the bed, stomped on it as it hit the floor and began to unpack my belongings.

That night around midnight when I returned to the cabin I had a twinge of fear. But as I filled my mind with what God had said earlier, I was able to rest fully in His peace. The retreat was blessed and many women were healed!

Encounters like this one strengthened my resolve to learn how to be able to hear God all the time. I was desperate and persistent and God rewards that kind of passion and desire. He means it when He says that He wants us to seek Him! Most of us think that if we seek God for a week, asking Him for something, we have done a big thing.

I am not saying that there is anything significant about the four-year intense timeframe that it took for me to have breakthrough. I am saying that this is the amount of time that it took me to really tune my ears to God.

Think about how lovers communicate. They talk for hours on the phone, spend days gazing into each other's eyes, and write love notes to each other. When we are consumed with love for God, we will take all the time in the world to get closer to Him.

"Be still and know that I am God" (Psalm 46:10).

To be still and then be still a little longer is a challenge for most people. When I find myself struggling with being quiet, I remind myself that all the things that seem more important than being with God will pass away. They are all temporary but He is eternal and, therefore, my priority. I focus on His sovereignty as Creator and King over all the earth and everything in it.

If you struggle with a busy mind or inability to concentrate, find Scripture to help you affirm God's rightful place as supreme ruler and deserving of attention and respect. *"How awesome is the Lord Most High, the great King over all the earth"* (Psalm 47:2).

The Key to Hearing from God

Have you ever attempted to tell God that you want to do whatever He wants you to do while thinking to yourself that you are afraid of what He might require? This is a trust issue. Will you trust God to know and do what is best?

"If anyone wills to do His will, he shall know" (John 7:17).

When our hearts and wills are submitted to God and ready to do whatever He directs — even before we know what it might be, His voice will be a constant companion! When you say, "Whatever Jesus leads me to do is what I am going to do," He will lead you. The willingness to act BEFORE God speaks is what attracts His voice!

If you want to hear God, you must first be willing to submit to whatever He might say to you. Fearing what He might say or do will not open the way to hear Him.

Your *Truster* May Need Healing

Almost every person has lost trust through life's circumstances and because of hurt caused by other people. And yet, being able to trust God is vital to hearing His voice and walking in victory. Asking God to heal your trust issues may entail letting go of structures that you have set up to protect yourself from being hurt again — risking hurt for the sake of faith.

Meditating on God's sovereignty helped me learn to trust Him in deeper ways. As I daily asked God to show me His bigness, and as I memorized Scripture about His greatness, my truster was healed.

God wants us to trust Him. Recently, I was asking God (again), "How can I repay You for Your goodness to me?" As I waited, I heard the voice of God in my heart speak, "Trust Me!"

One of the things that God greatly desires from His children is trust. We must trust that when we pray, we do not send wishes or thoughts out into the air. We send prayers to Heaven and to a living, listening and concerned Father who hears and answers!

> *"How can I repay the Lord for all of His benefits toward me? I will take up the cup of salvation and call upon the name of the Lord"* (Psalm 116:12-13).

Are you willing to eradicate any complaint you have against God? Are you willing to risk trusting Him with your life? Are you willing to risk trusting God with your future, your family and all that concerns you? It is up to you to ask God to heal your trust issues. Begin now to invite the Holy Spirit to reveal the places and times when you lost trust. When God reveals something, there is always remedy! God's voice reveals with remedy and freedom!

> *"Praise to the Sovereign LORD for His Creation and Providence; bless the LORD, O my soul! O LORD my God, You are very great: You are clothed with honor and majesty"* (Psalm 104:1-3).

Ask God to Silence Your Own Thoughts

We need help from God to hear Him. Ask God to silence your own thoughts, desires and the opinions of others which may be filling your mind. *"Take every thought captive to make it obedient to Christ"* (II Corinthians 10:5). King Jesus asks, *"How can you believe if you accept praise from one another, yet make no effort to obtain the praise that comes from the only God?"* (John 5:44).

Resist the Enemy

In order to hear God, you may need to resist the enemy. He may be lurking around, trying to deceive and scare you. Use the authority which Christ Jesus has given you to silence the voice of the enemy. Proclaim God's authority aloud in this way: "In the name of Jesus Christ and through His blood that has made me a child of God, enemy, be silent."

"Submit to God. Resist the devil and he will
flee from you" (James 4:7).

Then Jesus said to him, "Away with you, Satan! For it is
written, 'You shall worship the LORD your God, and Him
only you shall serve'" (Matthew 4:10).

What God Wants

The Lord desires to speak to you even more than you want to hear Him. Let's give God what He wants. As we do, the rewards of His presence and power will bring fulfillment that is real!

Expect God to Hear and Answer You

Expect an answer, submitting to God's way of answering you. Keep praying until you either have an answer or until you have been given grace to wait. There are times when this may take hours. Are you willing to persevere to hear from God?

"Answer me, O Lord, out of the goodness of Your love"
(Psalm 69:16).

"I wait for You, O LORD; You will answer,
O Lord my God" (Psalm 38:15).

"Get into the habit of saying, 'Speak Lord', and life will become a romance. Every time circumstances press in on you, say, 'Speak, Lord'
— and make time to listen."
Oswald Chambers, <u>My Utmost For His Highest</u>

If you are still having trouble hearing God, invite the Holy Spirit to search you and reveal any sin. Ask God to forgive you and to cleanse you from all unrighteousness. This is a prayer that God always answers!

"I cried out to Him with my mouth; His praise was on my tongue. If I had cherished sin in my heart, the Lord would not have listened; but God surely listened and heard my voice in prayer. Praise be to God, who has not rejected my prayer or withheld His love from me"
(Psalm 66:17-20).

Confirmation — Three Ways to Know That You Have Heard from God:

1. Does what you have heard point to Jesus Christ as LORD?

2. Does what you have heard line up with Scripture? God's voice never contradicts Scripture and will never make an exception for you to disobey the Scripture.

3. Does what you have heard fit with the "fruit of the Spirit" as stated in Galatians 5? (God's Spirit will always promote love, joy, peace, patience, kindness, goodness, gentleness, faithfulness and self-control — Galatians 5:22-23.

Does What You Believe to Be God Speaking to You:

- Stir you with love and devotion to Jesus Christ?

- Turn you away from your own wants and selfish ambition?

- Cause you to want to care for others?

For You to Pray:

Father God, I am sorry for the times that I have come to you for information only. I recognize that You want relationship to come first. Help me to know You for who You are. Please give me the desire to love You as You want me to love You. Thank You for loving me first!

PART TWO

MIRACLES BEGIN WHERE YOU ARE

For a follower of Jesus, every place is the right place and
every time is the right time for a divine encounter!

*Jesus said to them, "Go into all the world and preach the
gospel to every creature"* King Jesus (Mark 16:15).

Chapter 6

THE KEY TO TWICE AS MUCH

Wherever I go, people tell me they want breakthrough in their personal lives. Whether it is a promotion at work, a cure for illness, or the desire for satisfying, interpersonal relationships the hope for *more* cries out.

While ministering to pastors and leaders in India, I spoke about a principle that is critical to the well-being of people everywhere: prayer-cover. As we looked at Scripture and I told true stories of victories won through prayer support, I could feel the expectation rising in the room. I could almost hear the thoughts of the listeners, "If these victorious accounts of individuals who flourished because of prayer- protection are true, maybe there is hope for me." Then I gave forth these questions, "Do you want strong prayer support? Do you want to know how to obtain a personal intercessor who will pray diligently for you?"

Almost everyone in the room leaned forward, anticipating the answer to their need. In the quietness of that kind of breath-holding hope, I gave the answer, "If you want God to give you a personal intercessor, become one for someone else!"

The crowd visibly leaned back as each person realized that there was a price and that it would be a sacrifice. Then we made it doable. Instructing the men and women in that conference to pause for prayer, we came before Father God with listening hearts. I encouraged each individual to simply ask God, "Who?" And as we listened for God to speak, the atmosphere changed (as it does when people come before God in full surrender). The air was charged with the presence of the Holy Spirit and I saw the nods and heard the "yeses" as God spoke names to people and they agreed with Him.

The key to real fulfillment in life is prescribed by Jesus Christ, *"If anyone serves Me, [that person is who] My Father will honor"* (John 12:25-26). When we serve Jesus, we serve one another, and we are honored by God! Wow!

Right now, someone you know is in desperate need of your prayers. Through prayer, you can stand in the gap for them. You can influence the actions of an almighty and all-powerful God. As surprising as it is, this is the way the Lord chose to structure the way He works on earth. If we aren't praying, though, if prayer is missing, the full extent of God's power can be stifled. Prayer is the supreme instrument for releasing God's purposes into reality.

Praying for Others May be the Way to Find Breakthrough in Your Own Life!

One of the greatest examples of the personal benefit of praying for others is found in the book of Job. Scripture states that Job was restored and blessed when he prayed for his friends.

> *"The LORD restored Job's losses when he prayed for his friends. Indeed the LORD gave Job twice as much as he had before"* (Job 42:10).

Job was a man who had it all — servants, family, wealth, wisdom, good friends and a great relationship with God. Who could ask for more? Then suddenly, in one day, Job went through a terrible trial, losing all of his wealth, health and family. In reading the account of Job's life, we learn that he lost all he owned and loved, including his own dignity and health. Not only was Job in terrible pain and grief, but he had a group of *friends* who gathered to make him feel even more miserable.

Eventually, after much suffering, breakthrough came and Job was given twice as much as he had before.

It is interesting to note what the Bible says about the means to which the *"twice as much as he had before"* came (Job 42:10). Job was restored and blessed when he prayed for his miserable friends!

How did Job know that praying for his friends was the very thing that God wanted him to do? Through pain and suffering, Job became humble, open and honest. I also think that through the desperation that comes with suffering, Job was probably ready to obey God in anything He asked of him. Openness and obedience are keys to hearing from God. So is the willingness to forgive.

Job's friends needed grace. They had each spoken words to Job that caused him pain and could potentially sever their friendships. Forgiveness is almost always a part of moving forward in blessing. With forgiveness comes fresh love, and real love always includes prayer. People who will truly love God will pray.

The people who God asks you to pray for will need grace from you, too. To be a conduit of blessing for another person through prayer will require forgiveness and grace.

Many times as I have served as a personal intercessor for another person, I have been tempted to be offended. Maybe I did not feel appreciated *enough*, or I thought that the person for whom I was praying wasn't measuring up to my *sacrificial* efforts. The devil is always trying to stop prayer because it has such a powerful effect. We must be aware of the source of the temptation and be willing to battle the flesh and the devil!

Right Now, Someone You Know Needs Your Prayers

Steven Johnson, president of World Indigenous Missions, gives a great testimony to the difference prayer makes. "As president of a world-wide church planting ministry I found myself under severe spiritual attack. This resulted in extreme fatigue, the vexing of my soul, as well as spiritual attacks on my family."

So Steven formed a team of prayer partners for the first time. "Results of this were overwhelming," Johnson reports. "Within days of sending the letter, I sensed a tremendous lifting of spiritual oppressions.

I sensed a freedom concerning a warfare that was attacking my family as well as my personal ministry."

He attributes all of this to the power released by God through his prayer team. "I can give testimony to being significantly different than the months and years prior to having this prayer team." *No question exists in the minds of those who have experienced it; committed, faithful intercession brings increased spiritual power to Christians.*

Prayer Lists and Praying Leaders

Several years ago my husband, Tom, and I took a sabbatical from the church we pastored and went to a Discipleship Training School at a YWAM Base in England. There we met a pastor from Korea named Paul. As Tom began to build a friendship with Paul, they shared with each other about ministry and their churches.

One day Paul asked Tom the question, "Do you pray for your people?" Tom responded, "Of course I pray for my people." Paul pressed in, "Tom, I mean do you PRAY for your people?" To which Tom stated that, of course, he did. Paul continued to ask the question with even more fervency until Tom stopped him and asked, "Paul, do you pray for your people?" "Yes," Paul said, "Every day, each one by name."

Instantly Tom thought in his own mind, "Well, he must not have a very large church if he prays for every one of his people every day." So he asked, "Just how many people do you have in your church, Paul?"

Without hesitation, Paul replied, "I pray for over 600 people every day. I pray for my people."

That evening as Tom relayed this conversation back to me, I was stunned. I had never heard of such a thing. And, I wanted to know how Paul did it. We set a time to meet with Paul and his wife, Sarah, when we could ask them questions about how they prayed for so many people every day.

Over the course of the next several weeks, Paul taught us how to pray through a long list of people's names. He showed us how to call each name before the Lord while listening for the Holy Spirit's direction. (Sometimes the Lord wanted us to linger over a certain name before we moved on.) By the end of the sabbatical, Tom and I were lifting every person in our congregation (back home), before the Lord daily.

Since this time, we have served three other congregations, one with a list of nearly 1200 people, who we prayed for daily. (I have to say, as church planters, it has been a relief to start new churches where we only had to pray for a handful of people for the first few weeks. However, when you are praying for your people daily, your church is bound to grow! We now have a long list of people who we pray for daily here in Reno/Sparks, Nevada!)

What does the Lord do for a congregation of people who have pastors who pray for them daily? Miracles! It is written:

"For the eyes of the Lord run to and fro throughout the whole earth, to show Himself strong on behalf of those whose heart is loyal to Him" (II Chronicles 16:9).

God shows Himself strong, bringing blessing to those who pray for others!

You may not be a pastor or leader of a large congregation of people, but you most likely have neighbors, family members, and friends who need prayer. You can be an agent of blessing and help for those people as you pray for them.

Through the years, it has helped me to keep a prayer list of the people I pray for. In addition to the list of names of the people in our church, I have another list of people outside the church for whom I pray. Some are prayed for daily, others fall into different time categories, including once a week for my enemies! Yes, Jesus told us to pray for our enemies, too. I think this is what Job might have been doing at the point he was at with his miserable friends!

A Double Portion

Remember that Job got double from God after he prayed for others. Jesus Christ said, *"Whoever compels you to go one mile, go with him two"* (Matthew 5:41).

This teaching of the Lord is about doing more than what you have to do and *about giving more than is required.* It may not be your duty to go another mile past what someone asks of you, or to let someone slap you on both sides of your face (Matthew 5:39), but if you will do more than is required, you will receive more from God! Jesus said that if we love Him, we will obey Him. We will want to give more than is required.

We will not say, 'Oh well, I just can't do any more . . . Nobody else has to do so much." We will say, *"We are unprofitable servants. We have done what was our duty to do"* (Luke 17:10).

In this parable (Luke 17:5-10), the disciples were asking the Lord to increase their faith. Jesus asked a question about those who had already worked hard all day. He asked if they should come into the master's house and expect him to serve them. Then He answered the question with these words, *"Prepare something for my supper, and gird yourself and serve me till I have eaten and drunk, and afterward you will eat and drink"* (Luke 17:8).

The Lord expects us to serve others and give extra. He also expects us to serve Him first. Jesus went on to say:

> *Does [the master] thank that servant because he did the things that were commanded him? I think not. So likewise you, when you have done all those things which you are commanded, say, 'We are unprofitable servants. We have done what was our duty to do'"* (Luke 17:9-10).

How do we know when we have fully ministered to the Master? The intensifying of His pleasure sweeps us away in His Glory! And then we get filled with the glory and goodness of God; we get MORE!

God's goodness toward you and the glory of His presence go together. Remember that Moses cried out to God that he wanted to see His glory. What God showed Moses in answer to his prayer was His goodness.

> *The LORD said to Moses, "I will also do this thing that you have spoken; for you have found grace in My sight, and I know you by name." [Moses] said, "Please, show me Your glory." Then He said, "I will make all My goodness pass before you"* (Exodus 33:17-19).

Extra-Mile Lifestyles Bring Double Portions!

> *Elijah said to Elisha, "Ask! What may I do for you, before I am taken away from you?" Elisha said, "Please let a double portion of your spirit be upon me." So he said, "You have asked a hard thing. Nevertheless, if you see me when I am taken from you, it shall be so for you; but if not, it shall not be so"* (II Kings 2:9-10).

The prophet, Elisha, had to go the second mile in following Elijah around in order to get a double portion of anointing from him. Can you imagine altering your life-style to the point of following another person around wherever he or she would go? And yet, Elisha gave up his schedule and routine to get more by going the second (and third) mile!

What was the outcome? Elisha received more from God! Elisha received a double portion. The principle remains the same as when Jesus Christ spoke it, *"Give and it will be given to you ..."* (Luke 6:38).

What you need will come to you, but what you want you will need to go after. This is the time for going the extra mile.

When God laid out the plan for your life, He lined up the right people, the right breaks, and the right opportunities which you need to fulfill your destiny. But YOU have to pursue the divine moments of favor and moments of increase!

Be willing to engage in an impassioned pursuit of prayer; expect confrontation with the demonic, clear out anything that hinders your anticipation of the miraculous, acquire a burning heart for evangelism, look for those you can pray for, follow those who can help you, pursue the Father for deeper works of the Holy Spirit! Don't let this moment pass without making a commitment to God. Tell Him you want *more*!

Don't Let Yourself Get Bogged Down in Prayer

Oftentimes there are so many prayer requests from people that I can't keep up. Maybe you have felt this way or possibly even given up on praying for people because their needs weigh you down.

Recently, I was feeling over-burdened with needs. It seemed like I didn't have enough time for "sufficient" prayer for each request. I began to feel guilty for not giving each request more time and effort. I cried out to God for freedom as I recognized the burden of guilt that was becoming heavier and heavier. (I know that conviction is from God — but not guilt. Conviction is specific and lifts away with repentance. Guilt is general and doesn't lift with repentance.) As always, God heard my cry and gave me the solution in His Word!

"The Spirit also helps in our weaknesses. For we do not know what we should pray for as we ought, but the Spirit Himself makes intercession for us ..." (Romans 8:26).

As this Truth set me free, I wrote this in my journal: *"The Lord rescued me again! I have been under a burden of deception — so burdened in the last couple of weeks about praying for people. The needs are so vast and the list so long. I didn't feel that I was praying "enough" for anyone. Early this morning as I was praying through the list, the Lord spoke to me. He made clear that He hears every name lifted to Him and the Holy Spirit makes a paragraph out of my few words. Wow! The burden lifted completely . . . my heart sings with gratitude!"*

Your Prayers Matter to God!

Sometimes God will put a burden on your heart for someone and you will need to pray until the burden is lifted. But, most of the time, you will simply lift a person before God and ask for protection and blessing.

Note that I am not saying that you only need quickie-type prayers and that those kinds of prayers are always sufficient. I am saying that on top of your daily time of prayer, you will pray for people consistently and as long as the Holy Spirit leads.

> *"Pray without ceasing, in everything give*
> *thanks; for this is the will of God in*
> *Christ Jesus for you"* (I Thessalonians 5:17-18).

Who Will God Give You?

As you develop a plan for personal prayer ministry and have at least one person for whom you will intercede daily, you may ask, "Where is the person who will pray for me?"

Someone is probably waiting for an invitation from you! You will need to look around, wait for God to speak to you, and then, **ask** that person.

The Apostle Paul desired and asked for prayer cover:

> *"Brethren, pray for us"* (I Thessalonians 5:25).

> *"I beg you . . . that you strive together with me in*
> *prayers to God for me"* (Romans 15:30).

> *"I know that this will turn out for my deliverance*
> *through your prayer and the supply of*
> *the Spirit of Jesus Christ"* (Philippians 1:19).

> *"I trust that through your prayers*
> *I shall be granted to you"* (Philemon 22).

These Scriptures are directed toward asking a group of people for prayer support. You also, although you may not be an apostle like Paul, need and deserve prayer support. As you request to be prayed for, notice who responds back to you and who you know did indeed truly pray.

I have had several personal intercessors throughout my life and did not recruit any of them without a test. First of all, I request prayer from a group, a prayer chain, or from a ministry. I wait to see who follows up on my request with interest and concern. Then, I give that person a little bit more information and wait to see if there is further follow through. The individuals who have become my personal intercessors are people who have followed up on my prayer requests with true questions and concerns. Those who have a heart for me and truly seek my welfare are the ones who get my attention!

If you are a pastor or leader, please be very careful about who you invite into the inner circle of more detailed prayer for you. The devil will try to manipulate you into making poor choices of prayer partners. There are always people who desire to get close to a leader to gain recognition and power instead of the pure motive of loving prayer.

Take Time to Test it Out

After you have a sense that a certain person might be willing to commit to praying for you, test it out. Ask the person if he or she would be willing to receive your prayer requests for the next six weeks or so. Set a timeframe and see how it goes. As you give your requests to the individual, see if there is any change in the situations for which you have requested prayer. Note whether the intercessor follows up with you about how you are doing.

Make sure that you let the person who is praying for you know that he or she is appreciated. Send notes of thanks and give small gifts when appropriate.

In the past, I have frustrated my intercessor by not giving her my reports of answered prayer, or by not being diligent to send my requests (at least) weekly. A true intercessor, who is called by God to pray for you, will want to know what your specific prayer needs are.

My Heart

Several years ago I had a situation with my heartbeat that was distracting and annoying. For many months I had noticed that my heart would feel as though it were skipping a beat and then it would have a strong heartbeat that felt like it boomed through my chest and then skip around again. At times it was very pronounced and at other times it didn't bother me.

Eventually I saw my general practitioner about it and he referred me to a cardiologist. After several tests, the cardiologist determined that, for some unexplainable reason, my heart skipped every fifth beat. He suggested experimenting with medication, but other than that, he did not have an answer.

I had briefed Cheryl, who was my intercessor and prayer partner at the time, asking her to pray for my healing. Cheryl was diligent to pray for me, expecting God to heal me.

After the news that my heart was skipping every fifth beat, Cheryl asked that I give her enough time to pray for me (in person) until I was healed. I agreed and we set a date on the calendar.

The day came for the extended time of prayer. As I sat quietly in God's presence, Cheryl prayed for me for over two hours. During this time, I didn't experience anything unusual. There wasn't a lightning bolt or a special feeling. I simply submitted to faithful prayer and was grateful for the loving ministry. I remember leaving the setting that day, wondering what my heart would do in the days to come.

I have never had another known incidence of skipping a heartbeat! My heart was completely healed through the prayer of a loving intercessor! I am, to this day, astonished by this miracle and, oh, so grateful for God's healing through prayer!

Miracles and adventures are waiting for those who will serve others in prayer. What could be more fulfilling than partnering with God in the miraculous through prayer?

Get Ready to Be Captivated By Prayer!

Once you have prayed for a person, an event, or a nation and have seen confirmed answer to prayer, you are ruined for "normal" earthly life! Such is the thrill of intercession and the call of joining with God to see His Kingdom dominion come here on earth as it is in Heaven.

The words spoken to God about people in need, family issues, leaders and — well, everything, brings you into a wonderful love relationship with God. Coming before God, with prayers of faith and authority, affect blessing for other people and yourself. Prayer is the supreme instrument for releasing God's purposes into reality!

The Process: Slow and With Patience

- Ask the Holy Spirit to show you who He wants YOU to intercede for. After you get that name, begin to pray steadfastly for that person daily. After you have been faithful in prayer for that person for at least three months, you may be ready to take the next step.

- Connect with the person for whom you have been praying, either by mail, phone or in person. Let the person know that you have been praying for him or her and ask if there are any specific prayer needs.

- Wait and see what begins to develop as you continue to connect with the person for whom you are praying.

- Ask the Holy Spirit to show you who He is raising up to pray for you.

- Begin to test out that person through asking for prayer.

- Be patient in the process. God has a plan and you are fitting into His plan.

As a person of prayer, God gives you spiritual authority to pray for protection for those you love. Such is the unique place you have, whether you are praying for your family, your church, city or nation, people will receive certain victories and protection that they would not otherwise have because you pray! And you will have victories because God has raised someone up to pray for you. He will give you twice as much as you had before as you pray for your friends.

Questions

1. What is the name of the person for whom you feel led to begin to intercede for?

2. Who will you begin to test out to see if that person has a heart to pray for you?

3. Are you willing to commit to a process of prayer and waiting that may take several months?

4. Why do you think God required Elisha to follow Elijah around for a time before Elisha was doubly rewarded (see 2 Kings 2:9-10)?

5. Memorize John 15:13. For whom will you lay your life down (through prayer)?

For You to Pray:

Father God, Please create an excitement and anticipation in me for the good work that You will do in me as I determine to pray for others. Please give my name to someone who will pray for me every day! Thank You that You will! In Jesus' name, amen.

Chapter 7

PRAYER SHIELD

"I exhort first of all that supplications, prayers, intercessions, and giving of thanks be made for . . . all who are in authority, that we may lead a quiet and peaceable life in all godliness and reverence" (I Timothy 2:1-2).

People who are in leadership need prayer cover. All the way from the president of our nation, to your local church pastor, we are instructed to pray for people because, for one thing, prayer brings protection. Through prayer you can influence the actions of Almighty God, the One who set you up to be in partnership with Him!

Throughout Scripture we find that God listens when people cry out to Him. If we are not crying out to God for those in leadership over us, the full extent of God's power may be stifled in their lives. And, the peace God intends for us may be missing.

E.M. Bounds, who wrote much on prayer in the early twentieth century said, "Air is not more necessary to the lungs than prayer to the preacher."

Peter Wagner states, "The most underutilized source of spiritual power in our churches today is intercession for Christian leaders."

Spiritual power? What is that? In the natural realm it can be likened to getting on one of those moving walkways at an airport and suddenly you are moving super-fast! You are empowered by a force that propels you forward!

In the unseen realm whereas you may have been feeling sluggish or tired, spiritual power gives you energy and stamina!

Have you ever felt as though you were pushing against a stone wall when you tried to move forward in ministry? Prayer cover will dispense the resistance that the devil continually puts up in front of you.

When I was growing up, we had a concept in our church called "praying through". We were instructed to pray until we broke all the way through — which meant that one knew that change had really happened. Can you imagine the force of the breakthroughs that can occur when other people help to catapult you through roadblocks, further and faster, through their faithful prayer?

What Does a Prayer Shield Do?

Geese fly faster when they are in a formation that reduces wind resistance. The lead goose shields the geese behind it, giving ease of flight. Truck drivers know that driving behind (being shielded by) another truck will give them better gas mileage, as they have less wind resistance. The windshield on your car will keep bugs from flying into your eyes! A shield of prayer will increase your strength, protect you, and keep your sight clear!

Throughout our ministry, Tom and I have always enlisted prayer partners who pray for us daily. In order to be a leader on my ministry team, the applicant must commit to pray for me daily. Consequently, we have always had provision, church growth, and a solid marriage!

We truly believe that without prayer cover we would not be able to minister effectively for the Kingdom.

At Horizon Christian Church, we have a group of people who meet every Monday night to pray for the pastors. This group is called "The Pastor's Prayer Shield".

What Happened on a Plane in India

While writing this chapter, Tom and I had a great demonstration of how our shield of prayer works!

We travel to India every year to minister, speak at conferences and to visit The His Way Children's Home (our orphanage) in Bangalore. We were on a plane from New Delhi, heading for Bangalore, and when we were about 300 miles out of New Delhi, Tom noticed that the information screen on the seatback showed that our plane was turning around. He called it to my attention and we both became concerned that something was wrong. A few moments later, the pilot came on the intercom and announced that we had an "issue". For our safety, we needed to return to New Delhi. Needless to say, it was very stressful!

The flight crews swept through the cabin, commanding the passengers to put their seats upright, fasten their seat belts, and stow any articles or electronics that were being used. No other information was given. The flight crew then hurriedly took their seats, buckled in and the plane became deathly quiet.

Together Tom and I began to cry out to God, asking for protection. Immediately we remembered that what was happening right then, on a Tuesday morning in India, was coinciding with our Pastor's Prayer Shield prayer meeting back home on Monday night! It was the exact same time! We also remembered the prayer request list we had given the team before we left. At the top was "pray for an angelic escort for travel"! This realization gave us both amazing peace! The Lord flooded us with peace for the rest of the trip back and of course, we had a safe landing.

Later Tom commented that the entire plane and all the people on it were safe because of our Pastor's Prayer Shield praying back home in the States! We will know the full extent of this intervention when we see the replay in Heaven!

> *"For the eyes of the Lord run to and fro throughout the whole earth, to show Himself strong on behalf of those whose heart is loyal to Him"* (II Chronicles 16:9).

Where Do Miracles Begin?

If you have ever complained about a lack of miracles in your church, questioned why revival seems to tarry, or felt powerless to bring needed change, it could be that the issue is prayerlessness. Maybe the miracles will begin with you as you move forward in prayer for your pastor!

As we saw in the last chapter, if you want to be blessed, become prayer support for someone else. Right now, your pastor is in need of your prayers.

Following is the plan that the Holy Spirit gave to us for this vital prayer cover ministry.

The Prayer Shield Plan

Here are steps to how the prayer shield can get started in a church: A pastor of a church asks God to raise up and bring to the forefront true people of prayer. God answers by bringing in and raising up people in the church who have hearts to pray for their pastors. One of these intercessors, a person of vision (who has organizational skills), is appointed as the leader of the ministry.

The appointed leader recruits other people (six total, including them) and imparts the vision and passion. The primary prayer focus of these six individuals is to pray for the lead pastors and their families (see diagram).

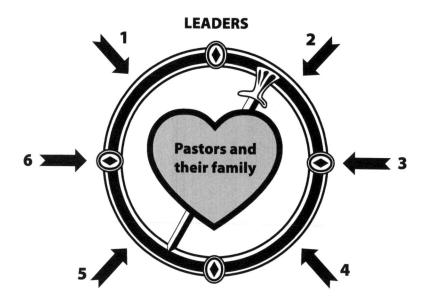

After this first circle of people is established and these leaders are meeting together regularly, twelve more people are prayed forward and recruited. These twelve new people become a circle of twelve people, surrounding the circle of six people. Of these twelve, two people will target (pray for) one person of the six, plus the pastors and their families.

Once this circle of twelve people is established and meeting together for prayer, the leaders scout out individuals for the next circle.

If you were to draw two more circles around the diagram, you would have three concentric circles, forming a round shield that protects the heart of the church!

At this point, this shield of prayer plan involves over 54 people (and may continue to grow). Imagine a church with people who pray for one another, the church and their pastors! Think what can be accomplished for the Kingdom of God in your city with this kind of spiritual strength!

Choosing People Who Will Pray

At Horizon, the individuals who were appointed for the first circle of six are people who we have watched and noted as people of character, prayer and loyalty. These six individuals have become our Pastor's Prayer Shield Core Team. They meet together every Monday night. The circles of people around them attend the prayer meeting every other Monday night.

Don't worry if it seems like there are not enough people who are mature intercessors to form your team. The primary characteristics that are needed include: loyalty, commitment, love and a teachable spirit! If a person desires to learn to pray, and you have asked the Lord if they should be included, go ahead and risk inviting that person to try it out. As with all ministries, there are always people issues. The benefits of this vital prayer ministry far outweigh the snags along the way!

Guidelines

To keep people committed and participating, it is best if the prayer meetings are structured to take place for one hour. Begin on time and dive right into prayer without small talk. The leaders should always come with a prayer list and guide the participants to stay on track. It helps if the pastors submit prayer requests to the leaders ahead of the prayer meeting. Make sure the meeting ends on time.

Sometimes the meetings open with a couple of worship songs. Diversity, according to the leading of the Holy Spirit (through the leaders), helps to keep the meetings from becoming stagnant.

Tom and I attend the PPS occasionally to thank the intercessors. We also attend when we need specific hands-on prayer support. The intercessors do not expect us to be there nor depend on us to be there.

A Graveyard for Pastors

When Tom and I moved to Reno/Sparks to plant a new church, many people came to us and all used the same words about our city, "This is a graveyard for pastors." Needless to say, we did not like these words, but we took them as a catapult toward doing something about this reputation — and saving our own skins!

We live in a city where many pastors have fallen into immorality, others have died in their prime, many have been divorced and many have just quit. The devil has had a plan to keep our city, called the "Divorce Capital of the World", as his territory. God has other plans for this city; plans to bless it and fill it with light and truth! The task is very difficult. We must have a strategy, and God has given us one.

The plan, not just for survival, but for growth and blessing, is our Pastor's Prayer Shield. Through the prayers of these people, we are strengthened and protected!

Is everything easy since we have such a great covering? Not yet. But, we are taking ground for the Kingdom and the purposes of God are going forward. With the prayer support and the fellowship of the Holy Spirit, we can scale this wall!

> *"For by You I can run against a troop, by my God*
> *I can leap over a wall. As for God, His way is perfect;*
> *the word of the Lord is proven; He is a shield to all*
> *who trust in Him"* (Psalm 18:29-30).

How Do We Mobilize So Many People to Pray for Us?

I believe that it goes back to what I shared in a previous chapter: we pray for the people of our church daily by name. As we pray for the people, God moves to bring blessing and raises up people to pray for us. Prayer begets prayer!

What Does God Want to Do Through You?

The chief way we are disloyal to God is to make small what He intends to make large through us. Let Him make something large, and larger through you as you join with Him in believing, world-changing prayer! You can pause right now and ask God what He wants you to do.

"Do not neglect the gift that is in you, which was given to you by prophecy with the laying on of the hands of the eldership. Meditate on these things; give yourself entirely to them, that your progress may be evident to all. Take heed to yourself and to the doctrine. Continue in them, for in doing this you will save both yourself and those who hear you" (I Timothy 4:14-16).

Questions

1. Do you ever feel frustrated because you want to see more miracles happen at your church?

2. Are you faithful in praying for your pastor and the pastoral staff of your church daily?

3. Do you believe that your prayers can be effective in moving your church farther into God's miraculous provision?

4. Pause and ask God what your part is in helping to create or serve on a prayer shield in your church.

For You to Pray:

Father God, please show me what Your plan is for my church, and then please show me what you want me to do to fit into Your plan. I am willing to step up to praying fervently for my pastor(s). Please give me strength to follow through, the love to inspire me and the passion to see Your Spirit move in miraculous ways! Thank You that You will!

Chapter 8

THE GOLDEN DOOR OF FASTING

We live in a time when more people are coming to know Jesus Christ as Lord than ever before! It is estimated that for an entire decade (the last ten years), at least 1200 people come to salvation every hour in the nation of China alone! There has never been such a time like this before as God is sweeping across the Earth and drawing people to Himself! And we are privileged to join with Him — and more than that, we can be used as catalysts to set in motion what He's doing.

One of the greatest ways in which we are the vehicles that set God's plans in motion is through subtracting food and adding in extra prayer!

As you read this chapter, get ready to close down the love affair with food for a time (and times) and set on fire your passion for God! Fasting is a grand adventure and well worth the sacrifice.

Fasting Rewards

"[Jesus] said to them, 'This kind [of unclean spirit] can come out by nothing but prayer and fasting'" (Mark 9:29).

Fasting has been a major emphasis in the lives of many of the great spiritual leaders throughout history. John Wesley, the founder of the Methodist denomination, fasted every Wednesday and Friday and required all of his clergy to do the same. Effective ministers of God from the apostle Paul to Martin Luther to Bill Bright made it a continual part of their walks with God.

You will need the power that comes through fasting in your life to be all that you desire to be for God. Whether you have been fasting for years or are just beginning, this discipline is vital!

If you are new to going without food for spiritual purposes, start slowly — fast for one meal in a day, or one day in a week, or one day in a month. Build up your spiritual muscles so that you will be prepared in a period of several months to fast for an extended time.

A concentrated time of prayer and fasting WILL have rewards that you will see and experience!

Anyone and Everyone

The late Bill Bright included this mandate in his list of how to bring revival to your church:

> *"Encourage all church members to fast and pray on behalf of the pastor and the church for one 24-hour period each week."*

Can you imagine what could happen in a church where ALL the members fast and pray like this every week? I believe that revival would take over our land and churches would be filled to overflowing!

Fasting is Not Just For the Super-Spiritual (Whoever *They* Are)!

Dr. Cho, founder of the world's largest church in Seoul, Korea states, "Normally I teach my people to begin to fast three days. Once they have become accustomed to three-day fasts, they will be able to fast for a period of seven days; then, they will move on to ten-day fasts. Some have gone for forty days, but this is not usually encouraged." Dr. David Yonggi-Cho, Prayer, Key to Revival

Having visited Dr. Cho's church in Korea, I can attest to the fact that God is moving in power in this praying nation! Their churches and prayer mountains are alive with people who are praying and fasting. As Tom and I have ministered at conferences in Korea, the people have almost worn us out with their fervency and prayer. Meetings go until midnight and the call-to-prayer bell sounds well before dawn!

An Expected Practice

The Bible speaks of fasting as if it is an expected practice. Instead of giving instruction as to how to fast, it simply records examples, within stories, about people who went without food at critical times.

Daniel denied himself *certain foods* for (at least) a three-week period in which he abstained from delicacies, meat and wine (see Daniel 10:3).

The Apostle Paul went on an abrupt fast for three days following his encounter with Jesus on the road to Damascus (Acts 9:9).

Moses and Elijah each engaged in a fast of forty days (Deuteronomy 9:9; I Kings 19:8), as did the Lord, Jesus Christ (Luke 4:2).

The king of Nineveh led his entire city to fast, including the dogs, cows and horses and the fast had huge rewards (Jonah 3:7-9).

Even a Pagan King Knew That Fasting Was the Answer

If you have lived on a farm or have a family pet, you know that animals begin to complain when they are hungry. A typically well-behaved dog may get into the garbage or destroy a household item if he is not fed. Can you imagine imposing a fast on your dog or cat?

This is exactly what the king of Nineveh did when the city was in danger — he called for a fast for all the people and the animals! No food and no water for any person or any animal.

"The people of Nineveh believed God, proclaimed a fast, and put on sackcloth, from the greatest to the least of them. Then word came to the king of Nineveh; and he arose from his throne and laid aside his robe, covered himself with sackcloth and sat in ashes. And he caused it to be proclaimed and published throughout Nineveh by the decree of the king and his nobles, saying, Let neither man nor beast, herd nor flock, taste anything; do not let them eat, or drink water. But let man and beast be covered with sackcloth, and cry mightily to God; yes, let every one turn from his evil way and from the violence that is in his hands. Who can tell if God will

turn and relent, and turn away from His fierce anger,
so that we may not perish" (Jonah 3:4-9?)

Do you think that there was the sound of horses whinnying, dogs howling and cows mooing across the land of Nineveh? The danger was so imminent and the situation so serious that sackcloth was worn by man and beast! What a picture and what a noise.

I often wonder why the leaders of nations in this our day do not follow the example of the king of Nineveh. The fasting had the power to turn away disaster. ***"Then God saw their works, that they turned from their evil way; and God relented from the disaster that He had said He would bring upon them, and He did not do it"*** (Jonah 3:10).

Our loving God will not resist a people who will turn to Him with cries for help, fasting and repentance!

Great People Know the Importance of Fasting!

The founder of Campus Crusade for Christ, Bill Bright, completed many forty day fasts in his lifetime. He wrote, *"Fasting is the most powerful spiritual discipline of all the Christian disciplines. Through fasting and prayer, the Holy Spirit can transform your life. Fasting and prayer can also work on a much grander scale. According to Scripture, personal experience and observation, I am convinced that when God's people fast with a proper biblical motive, seeking God's face not His hand — with a broken, repentant, and contrite spirit, God will hear from heaven and heal our lives, our churches, our communities, our nation and world."*

Bill Bright did not see fasting as a punishment, but rather as an opportunity to get closer to the Lord. Even though our bodies may rebel at first (and our minds may be opposing the concept right now), fasting is a dynamic discipline! The simple and central fact — fasting is something that you will only find out the reality and power of when you just do it!

Through fasting and prayer, the Holy Spirit can
transform your life.

Seeing the Invisible

"We do not look at the things that are seen, but at the things which are not seen" (II Corinthians 4:18). To be able to stick with a fast and keep yourself from running into the kitchen, a store or a restaurant after food, you will need to set your focus and persevere as those who see the invisible. In Scripture we find that the way that Moses endured, while waiting on the promise God gave him, was to look at the Invisible. *"Moses endured as seeing Him who is invisible"* (Hebrews 11:27).

What if, right now, before your eyes, you could see that by not eating food, there is a magnificent effect taking place?! You look down at your kitchen floor and see snakes and see that you are trampling them and they are dying (Luke 10:19)! Then, as you leave your house for errands, you notice workers building a mighty wall of protection around your home. You walk out to your car and see that there are four mighty angels, ready to escort you wherever you go, keeping you from harm. Then, as you go, singing praises to God, magnificent waves of light of indescribable color are flowing out of your mouth. And, as these waves go out and through other people, you see that they are healed, strengthened, and blessed!

These kinds of things ARE happening as you fast! These possibilities are enough to get you through a day of self-denial, are they not?

Benefits of Fasting

• **God Rewards Those Who Diligently Seek Him**

Some of God's rewards are spiritual and some are material. Job went through a terrible trial and yet he prayed, fasted and remained faithful. Job said, *"I have esteemed all of the words of His mouth more than my necessary food"* (Job 23:12). What is the end of the story of Job? God gave him *"twice as much as he had before"* (Job 42:10), both material and spiritual blessings. When you fast, you obey the Lord, and the Lord rewards obedience (Matthew 6:16-18).

• **Health and Healing Follow Fasting (Isaiah 58:8)**

Fasting helps physically by cleansing the body and giving the organs time to take a break. During the cleansing time that comes through fasting, you also get your soul cleaned — which heals your physical body too.

Since the devil works hard to inflame our emotions (offence, rejection, fear, insecurity, etc.), a concentrated time with God during a fast can actually reduce inflammation. Inflamed emotions often come through the *"flaming arrows of the evil one"* (Ephesians 6:16).

As you spend time with God instead of at the table, you will be shown where you need to forgive, where you need to let go of offence, and where any destructive emotion has gotten a foothold in your life. The Lord will faithfully show you where you have been inflamed because He wants you free and well.

There is much information these days about the destructive effects of inflammation. It seems that inflammation is the source of all kinds of maladies. As God's children, we know how to keep from getting any inflammation in us at all, don't we?! *"Above all, taking the shield of faith with which you will be able to quench all the flaming [inflaming!] arrows of the wicked one"* (Ephesians 6:16). TAKE UP YOUR SHIELD OF FAITH, deny yourself food and let God heal your inflamed emotions. You will feel better!

- **Fasting is a Biblical Way to Truly Humble Yourself in the Sight of God**

King David said, *"I humble myself through fasting"* (Psalm 35:13). Admitting that you are a person in desperate need of God will attract His attention. Just make sure that you are not getting attention from other people for your pious act! Remember that Jesus said, *"When you fast, do not be like the hypocrites, with a sad countenance. For they disfigure their faces that they may appear to men to be fasting. Assuredly, I say to you, they have their reward. But you, when you fast, anoint your head and wash your face, so that you do not appear to men to be fasting, but to your Father who is in the secret place; and your Father who sees in secret will reward you openly"* (Matthew 6:16-18).

- **There is Power in Corporate Fasting**

The Bible is full of true accounts of entire nations fasting for breakthrough. And guess what, the breakthroughs always took place! We are not powerless to effect change in the troublesome situations of life. There is a God in heaven who moves His hand when His people pray and fast together!

Fasting can result in a dynamic personal revival in your life and make you a channel of revival to others.

Prepared Through Fasting

A few years ago I was speaking at a retreat for a mainline denomination. On Friday evening the session went well and the Lord ministered to the women attending. Early the next morning, as I was preparing the messages for a long day of teaching, the Holy Spirit spoke to my heart and made it clear that I was to go without food. I immediately began to protest that it would be a long day and that I needed nourishment to make it through. "Besides", I told the Holy Spirit, "I am 'all fasted up'" (I fast weekly as a basic discipline). The Holy Spirit continued to impress on my heart that I must not eat. I eventually agreed and told God that He had to sustain me!

As I went into the morning session, things went well until almost noon. It was toward the end of the teaching time that a woman in the back of the room began to call out to me in an angry voice, interrupting my message. Immediately the Holy Spirit spoke to my heart that a demon was manifesting in this woman. I rebuked the demon and commanded it to be silent in the name of Jesus. Immediately the woman passed out. In an understandably responsible reaction, the retreat leaders scrambled to call 911 and get some help. I assured them emphatically that the woman was not having any kind of medical emergency and that we would deal with the demonic issue. I proceeded to finish the teaching quickly, dismissed the group for lunch and welcomed all who wanted to stay and pray. (Sadly, only one woman stayed as the room cleared rapidly.) For the next hour the Lord used me to bring deliverance to the woman. There was great victory and healing! That night, the newly-freed woman gave an incredible testimony and all Heaven broke out at that retreat!

Of course, the Lord knew what was going to take place and had prepared me through prayer with fasting. He also sustained me, just as He promised, as I obeyed His mandate to skip food.

Better Than Money in the Bank!

Just as a sensible person will open a savings account in a bank, preparing for a future expenditure; so a wise person will store up needed spiritual savings in their fasting bank! Have you ever felt like you were running out of spiritual energy? Maybe you need to store up some power in your spiritual bank account.

A good example of running out of spiritual power is demonstrated in the story of a boy who needed deliverance from a demon. The disciples of Jesus tried to help the boy but could not make the demon leave (Mark 9:17-18). When Jesus came, full of power and might, the demon left the boy and he was healed! No doubt the disciples felt rather sheepish as they asked the Lord what their problem was.

In verse 29 of that same passage, the Lord Jesus pinpointed the problem with these words: *"This kind can come out by nothing but prayer and fasting."* I don't think that the Lord was letting them know that they had eaten too much breakfast. I believe that He was talking about stored up spiritual power through a life-style of prayer and fasting!

The spiritual discipline of fasting is not easy and, sadly, far too few Christians are ready when challenging needs arise. Yet, we are instructed in the Bible to be ready at all times, *"in season and out of season"* (II Timothy 4:2).

Do you have family members or friends who need to be delivered through the power of God? Have you ever fasted as you diligently prayed for loved ones?

You can pause and take some time right now to ask God what He wants you to do in regard to getting some stored up power in your fasting bank. Are you willing to listen and obey what He might say to you?

Two Kinds of Fasting

You may observe two basic kinds of fasts: The general discipline and the special call of God.

The general discipline of fasting is the one that I have been practicing for many years. This means that I do not eat or drink anything (except water) for one or more meals one day each week. Besides the weekly day of fasting, as I sense the special call of the Holy Spirit, I will periodically observe extended days of fasting (as in the story I told of speaking at the retreat).

The Golden Door

Prayer is not something we do, prayer is somewhere we go. I can go to amazing places in the Spirit with God in prayer.

Fasting has been a golden door for me throughout my Christian life. During the times when insurmountable odds were against me, my family or the work of God in my ministry, I would close the door on my normal schedule and concentrate my focus fully on God. There has never been a single time in which I have earnestly sought God with all my heart that He didn't come through with His answers. God has never failed me. Not ever!

We are not powerless to effect change nor are we orphans. We have the opportunity, every one of us, to go after our loving Father for strategies, answers and solace. He is available and we must dispose of the clutter that takes our attention away from the larger purpose and picture — including the distraction of food.

Why does going without food capture Almighty God's attention? I hasten to say that going without food repairs our own attention spans! In an age when Attention Deficit Disorder is epidemic in children as well as adults, it is obvious that we need repair.

It would seem that being hungry, during a fasting and prayer time, would be a disturbance, as your stomach growls and your body craves food. Be encouraged that you can conquer the cravings and actually come to a place where food no longer rules your thoughts.

Take Scripture and fill your mind with words that will strengthen your resolve until you have victory over your own body.

> *"I run thus: not with uncertainty. Thus I fight: not as one who beats the air. But I discipline my body and bring it into subjection"* (I Corinthians 9:26-27).

> *"I have been crucified with Christ; it is no longer I who live, but Christ lives in me; and the life which I now live in the flesh I live by faith in the Son of God, who loved me and gave Himself for me"* (Galatians 2:20).

> *"It is the Spirit who gives life; the flesh profits nothing. The words that I speak to you are spirit, and they are life"* (John 6:63).

Let God dictate the outflow of your fast. Part of what happens to us is that we go into a prayer and fasting time with an agenda of what we want God to do. A fast should change our personal agendas into God's agenda until we emerge from the fasting time with a new perspective.

If we end the fasting time mad at God because He didn't do what we wanted, we haven't really sought the will of Heaven.

I remember one specific time when the Holy Spirit called me to fast and it didn't have the anticipated outcome in the natural. The fast was unexpected since I had completed a corporate fast for our nation a short time before, but I couldn't shake the sense that God wanted me to embark upon a "Daniel fast".

I researched the way that Daniel fasted and found that he had great favor as he subtracted choice foods from his diet (see Daniel 1:8-17, 9:3). I also found out that it took twenty-one days for a spiritual breakthrough at a critical time as Daniel prayed (Daniel 10:13).

Diligently seeking God, Daniel was given amazing insight from an angel and was greatly strengthened by God!

In obedience, I began a twenty-one day fast on a prescribed day. I ate no choice foods as my diet consisted of vegetables, water and grains. Although I did not know the purpose for which I was fasting, I trusted the Lord to help me pray daily for His purposes.

Please note the word "prescribed" in reference to the fast I was called to. The works God calls us to do, in union with His plans, were scribed (written) before we were born!

"For we are His workmanship, created in Christ Jesus
for good works, which God prepared beforehand
that we should walk in them" (Ephesians 2:10).

The prescribed twenty-one days of fasting was nearly over and the end was in sight. The only thing that I knew was that I felt noticeably stronger in my body and soul.

It was the twenty-first day and I was preparing to celebrate victory with delicious food, we got a phone call — our youth pastor had fallen into sin and what had transpired was coming out. The impact of that phone call cannot be overestimated as the sickening story began to unfold. But, the Lord had prepared me through fasting before this ordeal unfolded.

With a clear head and armed with strength, I was able to give wisdom and help to our staff and all the parties involved. The consequences of our youth pastor's poor choices were far less than they might have been and the repercussions and pain from the entire ordeal was diminished because of the preparedness through fasting.

Although I had no idea of what would take place at the end of my twenty-one days of fasting, the All-seeing God knew and had relief established through obedience. You might ask the question, "Why didn't God just stop the sin instead of initiating a fast?" God's way is to have a person stand in the gap for the sin of others (Ezekiel 22:30). He doesn't stop a person's free-will, but He does prepare the way for deliverance.

> *"For there is one God and one Mediator between God and men, the Man Christ Jesus, who gave Himself a ransom for all"* (I Timothy 2:5-6).

Our church recovered quickly from the pain and hurt that sinful choices caused. We were able to get through it with strength and with grace! I fully believe that the fasting had effect. Remember, we are not trying to make God move, but rather bring our spirits into alignment with His in order to be used by Him in our church, city, and nation.

As you fast, guard your heart against disappointment. If what you hoped for during a set-apart fasting time did not seemingly happen, take heart because you have raised up a foundation for many generations (Isaiah 58:12). The fasting that you do will plow up ground that will affect the generations to come! We don't just fast for ourselves, we fast for our children and grandchildren!

Although the twenty-one day fast that God called me to did not have the outcome for me personally of getting something material that I wanted, I reaped supernatural benefits! I was overwhelmed with the smile of God's approval and the joy of being used by Him.

The Lord can build upon us when He finds in us an inroad where He can work. Do not doubt the fact that He is at work!

As in the story of Daniel, it was days after Daniel's fast ended that an angel came (Daniel 10:4-5). Following your fasting times, go ahead and expect to have angel visitations in the future. But, don't stand staring at the sky waiting (Acts 1:11)! As we are about the Father's business, we shall have spontaneous, sudden times of hearing angels sing, of glimpsing Heaven, and of feeling the brush of angels' wings!

Remember the experience of the prophet, Daniel: *"From the FIRST DAY that Daniel began to fast, God heard"* (Daniel 10:12!)

What Will You Do?

Ask the Holy Spirit if He wants you to fast and the way that He wants you to go about doing it. God will answer you and then give you the strength to do what He asks! You will be amazed at the blessings you will receive from this important discipline!

Fasting is Something That You Will Only Really Know the Power of By Doing It! Verify Fasting Power By Fasting!

Disciplines for Power

As a pastor, one of the things that I hear most from people is, "I can't hear God." Usually this statement is made with an attitude of hopelessness. Through the years I have learned to ask a couple of revealing questions. I have found that the answers are always the same, "No, I am not spending time reading the Bible," and "No, I am not spending daily time in prayer and worship."

If we want to have the power of God flowing through us to touch the people around us, if we want to live fulfilled and joyful lives, if we want to hear God, we must practice the basic disciplines of life!

Even though I fast every Tuesday, it is always, every single week, a battle to surrender my desire for food (and I have been practicing fasting for decades)! But, each week I surrender to God because I know through experience the power and benefits of fasting. If I am going to be about the Father's business, the most fulfilling calling in the universe, I must discipline my body and fast and pray!

Real Bread

It is not easy to deny self of food, especially in the United States. We have more choices here than anywhere else on the planet — food is big business.

Consider how many magazines and TV shows we have about food. Think of the number of grocery stores and restaurants we have, all stocked to the top with food, food, food.

I have heard many missionaries tell about one of the things that is most difficult for them when they return home from the mission field to America — the choices that assail them. It is common for the act of going to a store here at home to be overwhelming for the just-home missionary.

The reason is this — other nations of the world do not have stores like we do; shopping is simpler. The countries I travel to (primarily India and South America) have small grocery stores with few food choices. No wonder Americans are obsessed with food when we have it in front of us at every turn.

Many Scriptures tell about God's people having an attitude about food — mostly a bad attitude — about what they did and did not have to eat.

> *"We remember the fish which we ate freely in Egypt, the cucumbers, the melons, the leeks, the onions, and the garlic; but now our whole being is dried up; there is nothing at all except this manna before our eyes!"* (Numbers 11:5-6)

This list of foods that the children of Israel wanted always makes me laugh (leeks, onions, cucumbers). These are not the foods I would complain about. I would be more prone to feel deprived if I couldn't have pizza or cookies. My taste buds holler for tasty treats and God knows I need to conquer these temptations.

While fasting we silence the grumbling of the stomach (and taste buds) with the unhindered presence of the Holy Spirit. Only God abiding in our lives can satisfy our inner longings. Only one real Bread of Life is always available; Jesus said, *"I am the bread of life"* (John 6:32, 48!)

May we all, as God's people, be filled with purpose, faith and the passion to fast and pray! We are going to win something great through denial of self. At this time cool and casual Christianity will not do. Our city (and nation) urgently needs the life-giving message of the Cross through us!

Fasting Will Prepare You For Blessing

The act of the spiritual fast will bring blessing to your life that may not have come otherwise.

* Fasting will break poverty from your life

- Health and healing will begin through a fasting time

- Fasting will overcome addictions and demonic powers

- God will bless your family and children because of your fast

Be assured that God will hear you and He will answer. Also recognize that although God heard Daniel's prayer on the first day he began to fast and pray, it took twenty-one days for the answer to come. Daniel persevered and so must we.

Are You Ready?

What will you do with the discipline of fasting? Pause and let God know that you are willing to fast if He wants you to. Then ask Him what He wants you to do. Wait for Him to speak to you and then write down what He said. He is a God who speaks and you can hear Him.

Your concentrated time of prayer and fasting WILL have reward that you will see and experience here, now, and in Heaven. When we sit around the great screen in heaven and watch the video of our fasts, we shall see the AMAZING effect our prayer and fasting had on our lives, churches and world! I can't wait to see this replay!

Questions

1. Please read Matthew 17:14-21. What do you think was the reason why the disciples could not cast the demon out of the boy?

2. Do you have family members or friends who need to be delivered through the power of God?

3. Have you ever fasted as you diligently prayed for loved ones?

4. What did the Lord say that you are to do when you fast (according to Matthew 6:17)?

5. Take some time to ask God what He wants you to do in regard to fasting at this time in your life. What did the Lord say?

For You to Pray:

Father, please help me to be willing to fast and to become a person who You can call to fast any time You want to. Help me to commit one day each week and then to follow through with denying myself food as I diligently seek Your face. I am ready for this new adventure and will, by the power of Your Holy Spirit, become a person who helps to bring Your Kingdom purposes to Earth!

Chapter 9

DISMANTLING STRONGHOLDS

Most everyone has at least one area in their life where they have set up their own thoughts above God's Word. These thought patterns are called "strongholds" and need to be dismantled in order for us to live successful lives.

Destructive thought patterns can bring about sickness, loss, and can actually stop the work of God through us.

As you read this chapter, you will have the opportunity to identify strongholds that reside in you and learn how to minister truth to others the truth that will set them free!

Jesus Christ stated, ***"You shall know the truth, and the truth shall make you free"*** (John 8:32).

Have You Ever Heard Someone Say That They Keep Doing the Same Destructive Things Over and Over Again?

Patterns of thought that lead to action reside in all of us. A woman may be a worry-wart, living with dread about all the *what ifs* of life. A man may be explosive, always on the edge of blowing up. You may struggle with unbelief, often questioning and disputing in your mind about God's goodness and love. Almost everyone has at least one area that God is working on to bring His truth into at any given time.

Francis Frangipane wrote, *"Rare is a Christian who is not limited by at least one of the following strongholds: unbelief, cold love, fear, pride, unforgiveness, lust, greed, or any combination of these, as well as the possibility of many others. Because we excuse ourselves so readily, it is difficult to discern the areas of oppression in our lives. After all, these are our thoughts, our attitudes, our perceptions—we justify and defend our thoughts with the same degree of intensity with which we justify and defend ourselves."* <u>The Three Battlegrounds</u>

Take the Short Route

Recently, while listening to Exodus 13:17-18, I heard: ***When Pharaoh had let the people go, God did not lead them by way of the land of the Philistines, although that was near; for God said, "Lest perhaps the people change their minds when they see war, and return to Egypt." So God led the people around by way of the wilderness of the Red Sea.***

I wondered why at this particular time, God's people did not have to see war, but many other times they had to fight.

Eventually, God gave me an answer. Because of His grace; He only leads us into the battles that we are prepared to win!

In His grace, God knew that the people of Israel were not prepared (mature) enough to win the battle so He took them another route. They missed the shorter road because of immaturity. It was God's kindness toward undeserving people that delayed their progress!

This understanding scared me. I saw clearly that the places of my own immaturity and the strongholds that I hold onto may keep me from the shorter route and my full potential.

The Holy Spirit gave me deeper understanding while studying Exodus 33:2-5. The LORD said to Moses, ***"Depart and go . . . I will send My Angel before you, and I will drive out the [enemy]. Go up to a land flowing with milk and honey; for I will not go up in your midst, lest I consume you on the way, for you are a stiff-necked people."***

God sent His Angel *before* the people, not *with* the people. God was protecting them because the intensity of His Glory might kill them; they were not strong enough to walk in the intensity of God's glory. Only a holy people can stand the intensity of God's glory!

While reading this, I thought of Ananias and Sapphira (Acts 5:1-10). The glory of the Lord was so great during the time of the early church that those who got close to IT were in danger — if they had strongholds of sin. On this occasion, the strongholds were love of money, image (wanting to appear more than they were) and lying.

We can get waylaid because of sin. In Israel's history, the entire community of believers had to take the longer route, even the die-before-you-get-there route, because of their stiff necks. God is too good to let us experience the glory that our stiff necks cannot stand.

In God's loving-kindness and grace, He even protects us from the very thing that we beg for: His glory. No one can stand in His glory without holiness. *"Without holiness, no man shall see God"* (Hebrews 12:14).

God protects us from seeing Him because He loves us too much to give us more than we can handle in our sinful state. Consequently, the glory (God's goodness and radiance) that we so desire is often lacking in our midst. How can we get free and how do we live in God's glory?

Our Mindsets Can Keep Us From Experiencing the Great Things of God

Wanting to see God's glory can propel us toward being willing to dismantle strongholds. We are willing to change our thinking when we realize that our own minds can keep us from experiencing the great things of God.

In Jesus' ministry, as He went into Nazareth and ministered the Good News, people began to be healed. And yet the people in the temple said, "Wait a minute, we know this man. We know his upbringing; we know his brothers; we know the family. How is it that these words of wisdom can come from him and these signs should follow?" They were intellectually offended. Their minds shut down their capacity to receive from God and their reasoning shut down the anointing on the Son of God Himself.

Mental offense and unbelief closed down the anointing in the temple where Jesus was present to minister. And the conclusion was that Jesus could do no mighty works there except to heal a few sick people.

"Now [Jesus] could do no mighty work there, except that He laid His hands on a few sick people and healed them. And He marveled because of their unbelief. Then He went about the villages in a circuit, teaching" (Mark 6:5-6).

A person's thought-life, where strongholds of unbelief, skepticism, offense, etc. can reside, may be in contradiction to the truth of God's ways and word. What happens when our thought life is in contradiction to what the Holy Spirit wants to do? Nothing!

Luke 5:17 tells us that *"the power of the Lord was present to heal them."* The *them* were the Pharisees and teachers of the law. There must have been some of *them* that needed healing. But no one was healed, even though there was power present to heal them. Jesus asked them the question that revealed their block: *"He perceived their thoughts and said, 'Why are you reasoning in your hearts?'"*

These people of Nazareth witnessed in their hearts. They marveled at His words — words filled with grace to each individual. The people had revelation, but then they allowed a question to undermine their revelation.

"When you are in the middle of a bad day . . . Aim your hard questions at God, not man. Why? Because in life's darkest hours, there are usually no human beings with adequate answers. Counselors may analyze, associates may sympathize, and experienced friends may empathize. But finite minds and feeble flesh can never satisfy us with the Presence we seek, for we truly cry for God Himself, not answers." Jack Hayford, How to Live Through a Bad Day

Do Your Questions Lead You to God or Away From God?

There is a big difference between asking God questions and questioning God. The former will lead you closer to Him, while the latter will close down communication. The devil is continually tempting people to question the character and reality of God.

Let's say a man (we will call him Joe) is walking along in victory. Joe is feeling blessed and encouraged when out of the clear blue sky, an unbelieving thought pops into his mind. It is as though Joe is walking along with the Lord, holding onto His hand and believing His word, when the devil comes up from behind and says something like, "You really can't hear God." The next thing Joe knows, he is repeating the devil's lie, "I can not really hear God." In buying into this suggestion, it is as if Joe drops the Lord's hand and takes hold of the devil's hand. Then later Joe is wondering why he feels confused and depressed.

If Joe were to recognize the lie that he allowed to take root in his mind, and then replace the lie with the truth found in Scripture, he would be able to resist the devil and the devil would have flee!

"Submit to God. Resist the devil and he will flee from you. Draw near to God and He will draw near to you. Cleanse your hands, you sinners; and purify your hearts, you double-minded" (James 4:7-8).

Strongholds are formed when the devil's lies are held onto instead of being dealt with as the Bible instructs. To be effective in finding freedom from strongholds for yourself and in helping others come into that wonderful place of freedom, you will need to know the truth!

The following instruction and the examples on the next few pages will give you understanding and revelation. Be sure and open your heart to the conviction of the Holy Spirit as you read.

Coming Into Agreement With God's Word of Truth

"We demolish arguments and every pretension that sets itself up against the knowledge of God, and we "take captive every thought to make it obedient to Christ" (II Corinthians 10:5).

Satan's Mind Strategy

How the Tempter Tries to Deceive a Person in His or Her Thought Life

Since the beginning of time, Satan has been tempting people to discount God's Word. We know how he works because God gave us a clear pattern in Genesis 3:1-5:

Question God's Word   "Did God really say . . .?" Genesis 3:1
Deny God's Word   "You will not surely die." Genesis 3:4
Replace God's Word   "And you will be like God . . ." Genesis 3:5

First of all, Satan tries to get us to <u>question God's Word</u>; *"Did God really say . . .* (Genesis 3:1)?

If we begin to doubt God, Satan can then plant ideas that <u>refute (deny) God's truth</u>; *"You will not surely die"* (Genesis 3:4).

Next, the devil gives us thoughts that sound so logical that we may <u>re-place God's Word with a lie</u>: *"And you will be like God . . ."* (Genesis 3:5).

The tempter, Satan, continues to speak lies into the minds of people today in the same way he did with Adam and Eve. This is how deception takes place.

"Now the serpent was more crafty than any of the wild animals the LORD God had made. He said to the woman, "<u>Did God really say</u>, 'You must not eat from any tree in the garden' ? ""The woman said to the serpent, " We may eat fruit from the trees in the garden, but God did say, 'You must not eat fruit from the tree that is in the middle of the garden, and you must not touch it, or you will die.' "<u>You will not surely die</u>,"" the serpent said to the woman. "For God knows that when you eat of it your eyes will be opened, and <u>you will be like God</u>, knowing good and evil. "When the woman saw that the fruit of the tree was good for food and pleasing to the eye, and also desirable for gaining wisdom, she took some and ate it. She also gave some to her husband, who was with her, and he ate it" (Genesis 3:1-6). NIV

Read carefully through the following examples that will help you recognize destructive thought patterns. Scriptural truth is given to counter each lie and the remedy is sure.

<u>Question</u>	**"How could God love me?"**
<u>Deny</u>	"God doesn't care about me."
<u>Replace</u>	"If I try harder to do good things, I can gain love."
Truth	**John 15:9: *"As the Father loved Me, I also have loved you; abide in My love."***

<u>Question</u>	**"Is there any point in praying for healing?"**
<u>Deny</u>	"God doesn't care about me."
<u>Replace</u>	"People were healed in the Bible, but God doesn't heal nowadays."

Truth	**Hebrews 13:8:** *"Jesus Christ is the same yesterday and today and forever."* **James 5:15:** *"Is any one sick? Prayer offered in faith will make the sick person well."*
Question	*"Did God really say that I must love my spouse?"*
Deny	"God (who is supposed to be so good) could not expect me to stay in such a difficult marriage and waste my life."
Replace	"God wants me to be happy, and I will only be happy if I get out of this situation."
Truth	**I Corinthians 7:10:** *"To the married I command, yet not I, but the Lord, let not the wife depart from her husband."* **I Corinthians 7:39:** *"The wife is bound by the law as long as her husband lives."* **Colossians 3:19:** *" Husbands, love your wives and do not be bitter toward them."*
Question	*"How could God expect me to love a person who is mean to me?"*
Deny	"God knows that I can't forgive such an awful person."
Replace	"I will just ignore her (him) – that is the best I can do."
Truth	**Matthew 5: 43, 44:** *"You have heard it said, 'You shall Love your neighbor and hate your enemy.' But I say to you, love your enemies, bless those that curse you, do good to those that hate you, and pray for those who despitefully use you."*
Question	*"How could God use people to write the Bible without any mistakes at all?"*
Deny	"The Bible can't be all true."
Replace	"I will just choose what I can believe and not worry about the rest."
Truth	**II Timothy 3:16:** *"All Scripture is given by inspiration of God, and is profitable …"*

Question	***"Why didn't God give me talents like others?"***
Deny	"God did a lousy job when He made me."
Replace	"I will let someone more capable do the job."
Truth	**Philippians 4:13: *"I can do all things through Christ who strengthens me."***
	Jeremiah 1:7: *[The Lord said] "Do not say, 'I am only a child.' You must go to everyone I send you and do whatever I command you."*

Question	***"Does God care that I am all alone?"***
Deny	"God won't help me. He is so far away."
Replace	"I will have to take care of myself."
Truth	**Hebrews 13:5: *"I will never leave you or forsake you."***
	II Corinthians 1: 3,4: *"The God of all comfort who comforts us in our troubles."*

Question	***"How can Jesus be the only way to Heaven?"***
Deny	"Many roads lead to God."
Replace	"I am fine with all the gods and feel that people should worship whoever they choose to."
Truth	**John 14:6: *Jesus Christ said, "I am the way, the truth and the life. No one comes to the Father except through Me."***

Do You Have an Example in Your Own Life?

Now that you have read the examples of the way in which strongholds get set up in your mind, pause and ask the Holy Spirit to identify any hidden strongholds in you.

"If you want to identify the hidden strongholds in your life, you need only survey the attitudes in your heart. Every area in your thinking that glistens with hope in God is an area which is being liberated by Christ. But any system of thinking that does not have hope, which feels hopeless, is a stronghold which must be pulled down." Francis Frangipane, The Three Battlegrounds

The process of renewing your mind is a lot of work, but so worth the struggle! When I learned to capture my thoughts and make them obey the truth of Scripture, my entire life changed.

When I was upset with my husband, instead of meditating on negative thoughts, I forced myself to think on Proverbs 14:1: *"A wise woman builds her house, but with her own hands, a foolish one tears hers down."* Then I would instruct my soul, "You will not tear this house down!"

When I would feel the weight of indefinable guilt, I'd meditate on Romans 8:1, and declare that there is no condemnation for me because I am in Christ Jesus! (Guilt and condemnation are always nebulous and vague. Conviction from God is always specific and comes with remedy.)

Is it possible to capture EVERY thought and make EVERY thought obey God? I believe it is possible, because we are instructed in God's Word to do it. We are not given commands that we cannot obey. However, I do believe that the process of learning this discipline is life-long.

Renew Your Mind with God's Word

The process of renewing your mind and washing it with the Word of God (Ephesians 5:26) is so important! To keep yourself from thoughts that will make you sick, depressed or cause you to fall into sin:

1. **DECIDE** how you will think:

"I will not buy into any idea that is contrary to the Bible. I will learn to catch all the bad thoughts the devil puts in my head and drive them out. I will consciously set my mind on God's Word and think on things that are good."

"Whatever things are true, whatever things are noble, whatever things are just, whatever things are pure, whatever things are lovely, whatever things are of good report, if there is any virtue and if there is anything praiseworthy — meditate on these things" (Philippians 4:8).

"Casting down arguments and every high thing that exalts itself against the knowledge of God, bringing every thought into captivity to the obedience of Christ" (II Corinthians 10:5).

2. ASK GOD to help you:

Father, please help me to think on Scripture instead of daydreaming or dwelling on unpleasant episodes in my life. Help me to remember that all my thoughts are open to You and therefore I won't surprise or horrify You with what I am thinking. You will help me! Please encourage and strengthen me with pure thoughts!

> **"Let Your hand become my help, for I**
> **have chosen Your precepts"**
> (Psalm 119:173).

3. WRITE OUT SCRIPTURE and memorize it:

Copy and carry Bible verses with you. Use spare moments or times when your thoughts are troubled to remind yourself to take out the words and read them. If possible, memorize the Scripture. Let the words penetrate deep into your spirit. Fall asleep thinking on Scripture. Purchase some Scripture music, the Bible on CD or MP3 and listen to it.

> **"I remember Your name in the night,**
> **O LORD, and I keep Your law"**
> (Psalm 119:55).

4. BEGIN TODAY to work on getting rid of strongholds

Here is a simple daily plan to work on your thought life:

Open your Bible and get some paper and a pen

Ask God to show you your need

Believe He will speak to you; God has just heard you talk to Him

Write down the need or issue that you have been shown

At first you may hear words in your mind that are not from God. They may be something like, "I can't hear God" or "The Bible may not be true" or any other words that cast doubt on God's love for you and/or make you feel hopeless. Go ahead and write the thought down — but after you write it, cross it out and write "untrue" over it! Ask God to open your eyes to the truth in His Word and continue on.

"Everyone who is of the truth
hears My voice" (John 18:37).

As you begin this process, you may want to select one of the following passages to read in your Bible:

Depression — Psalm 25

Fear or Doubt — Isaiah 43

Worry — Matthew 6 (beginning with verse 25)

Judging Others — Luke 6 (beginning with verse 27)

Overcoming Guilt — Romans 8

Faith — Hebrews 11

Trials and Temptation — James 1

Praise and Worship — Psalm 19 and 100

- Read only until God speaks to you

- Receive from God what He wants you to know

- Record what you learned in your notebook or journal

- Thank God for His goodness to you

As you go about your day, continue to remind yourself of what the Holy Spirit has shown you and how He will help you.

"Your heart is a fertile greenhouse ready to produce good fruit. Your mind is the doorway to your heart — the strategic place where you determine which seeds are sown and which seeds are discarded. The Holy Spirit is ready to help you manage and filter the thoughts that try to enter. He can help you guard your heart. He stands on the threshold. A thought approaches, a questionable thought. Do you throw open the door and let it enter? Of course not. You "fight to capture every thought until it acknowledges the authority of Christ" (II Corinthians 10:5). You don't leave the door unguarded. You stand equipped with handcuffs and leg irons, ready to capture any thought not fit to enter." Max Lucado, Just Like Jesus

Questions

1. Do you have an example in your own life or where the tempter's lies have caused you to question, deny and replace God's Word of truth?

   Your Question:

   The temptation to deny and replace:

   Truth found in God's Word for you:

2. According to 2 Timothy 2:15, how can you know the difference between truth and the philosophy of the world?

3. The Lord has given you divinely powerful weapons for the destruction of strongholds (see II Corinthians 10:4). What is your plan of action to use these weapons?

For You to Pray:

Father, I want to walk in Your truth. Please expose the lies that I have believed and that I have given place to. Help me to meditate on Your Word and fully wash my mind until it is renewed. I welcome Your conviction daily as You work to bring me into complete freedom. Thank You for loving me and that You will bring me into a place of a renewed mind. In Jesus' name, amen.

PART THREE

MIRACLES BEGIN WITH COURAGE

God wants you to ask Him and believe Him for things that are bigger than yourself. He wants to use you to jar the people around you into the reality of His Presence. Wherever Jesus went, there was a continuous supernatural flow of miracles. This very same Jesus resides in you!

"When they saw the boldness of Peter and John, and perceived that they were uneducated and untrained men, they marveled. And they realized that they had been with Jesus" (Acts 4:13).

Chapter 10

Wisdom in Dealing with the Demonic

Then Jesus answered and said to them, "Most assuredly,
I say to you, the Son can do nothing of Himself,
but what He sees the Father do; for whatever He does,
the Son also does in like manner" (John 5:19).

Jesus Christ only did what He saw His Father doing. He never tried to make Himself look good. He never chased a demon to show His power. Jesus Christ watched the Father and moved His hand in perfect synchronization with Him.

When we step out to bring deliverance to a person, we must know if God is moving that direction. Unless God is at work, we will lack power and put ourselves in jeopardy.

When We Step Out to Bring Deliverance to A Person, We Must Know if God is Moving That Direction

One afternoon I was ministering in a city where my dear grandmother lived. I was looking forward to visiting her after I finished speaking and praying for people. As I was getting ready to leave the meeting, I noticed a woman waiting for me in the back of the room. She had not come forward for prayer, but had waited until I was about to leave before she approached me. The woman had marks on her arms from burning herself, and seemed to be in great need of deliverance from tormenting spirits.

After almost two hours of dealing with her, I quit trying and left her. I felt like Jesus' disciples must have felt when they couldn't cast out a demon (Mark 9:28).

I was so late to see my grandmother (she was very worried about me, and upset when I finally did arrive). I apologized to my grandmother and we spent time together, but the questions about the woman at the meeting were in the back of my mind, "Why could I not cast out the demons?" "What did I need to learn?"

As I sought the Lord about this incident, He showed me that this woman had been used to delay me and keep me from honoring my grandmother (as well as wear me out). The Lord had not walked over to the woman, I had walked over on my own. In Matthew 7:6, the Lord instructs us, *"Do not give what is holy to the dogs; nor cast your pearls before swine, lest they trample them under their feet, and turn and tear you in pieces."* I had allowed the pearls of time with my grandmother to be stolen by not "watching what my Father was doing."

From this incident, the Lord taught me several things that have since increased my wisdom:

- When someone waits purposefully to be the last one to have my attention, they may be trying to take control of my time

- I am to ask the question in the beginning, "What do you want God to do?" If there is no expressed desire for God to work, He may not be working there

- The battle is first won in my secret time alone with God, never in public. I must daily ask God to show me where He is at work and then pay close attention

Obstacles and Wisdom

When you step out in faith to help people, expect the forces of darkness to oppose you — but don't let them stop you! Be wise and recognize the (tactics) of the enemy. He will try specific ploys to try to distract and delay your ministry.

"Let us not be ignorant, lest Satan should take advantage of us; for we are not ignorant of his devices" (II Corinthians 2:11).

Be Prepared to Recognize These Ploys of the Devil:

- **Spirit of Manipulation:** A person oppressed by this spirit is looking for sympathy and excuses for their *lot in life*. They do not want deliverance; they want to keep you from ministering to others by manipulating your time and stealing your sympathy.

- **Theatrical Spirit:** A person oppressed by this spirit will make a big scene with crying, yelling, or thrashing around. Bind the theatrical spirit in the Name of Jesus and tell it to be silent. If the person continues to put on a show, instruct them to stop and make it clear that you are aware of the tactic.

- **Spirit of Flattery (Python):** This spirit will try to steal your time by appealing to your human need for affirmation. Do not listen to flattery, nor stop and give it time. (The Apostle Paul dealt with this spirit — Acts 16:16-18).

- **Spirit of Intimidation:** This hindering spirit will try to keep you from ministering to other people by causing you to feel that you have nothing to offer. It will get in your path and express a fabricated or exaggerated problem. When you try to deal with this issue, you will begin to feel that you are powerless. Since the issue is a distraction, there is no way to solve the issue. You will begin to feel that since you can't help this person, you can't help anyone. Use II Timothy 1:7 as your sword and move on.

"For God has not given us a spirit of fear, but of power and of love and of a sound mind" (II Timothy 1:7).

Be Willing to Help People

You will encounter demons that you must deal with if you want to help people. Jesus never sent anyone out to preach the Good News without specifically instructing them and equipping them to take action against demons. Jesus leads us by the examples we read in the Bible about His earthly ministry. We must be willing to minister as He did (and still does through us!).

"Then [Jesus Christ] called His twelve disciples together and gave them power and authority over all demons, and to cure diseases. He sent them to preach the kingdom of God and to heal the sick . . . Behold, I give you the authority to trample on serpents and scorpions, and over all the power of the enemy, and nothing shall by any means hurt you" (Luke 9:1; 10:19).

Jesus Christ told us that we would do greater things! This includes casting out demons.

"Most assuredly, I say to you, he who believes in Me, the works that I do he will do also; and greater works than these he will do, because I go to My Father" (John 14:12).

In order to help bring freedom to people and to advance the Kingdom, we need wisdom and we need to be willing. Although I have had troubling encounters and situations where I was humbled, I will continue to do all that I can to help other people find freedom in Jesus Christ!

I often read a quote from John Osteen to inspire and motivate me:

"There are thousands of people held by demonic powers, witchcraft, and doctrines of devils because they have been denied the supernatural power of God . . . every child of God should be a channel of the supernatural energy and the divine gifts of the Holy Ghost."

We need willingness and wisdom as we are about the Father's business of setting people free from demonic influences!

One of the times when I was not wise "enough" and ended up being hurt was several years ago when Tom and I were ministering in the Yucatan. We were in a village ministering at a small church where we had been used by God to bring many miracles of healing. The small congregation had swelled to well over a hundred people as villagers heard about the healing power of Jesus and came to be healed.

Because of the great miracles that God was doing through us, I became careless and began to feel invincible in ministering. I didn't follow the important guidelines that I teach others to follow — like praying in partnership with other people.

It was the last night of the meetings and a young woman who had been delivered of many demons was sitting next to me. She was noticeably changed as she had been unable to speak when we first arrived and was now able to communicate. I did feel that she was wanting to hold onto some of the demonic power that she previously had though, and hoped she would be fully freed.

During the service the young woman began to manifest demonic activity as her body began to convulse. Of course I noticed and put my hand on her, commanding the demonic activity to cease. The young woman jerked away and ran out of the church and into a small dark structure (lean-to) outside.

Normally I would not follow a person who was manifesting a demonic spirit by myself. But because of so much successful ministry, and having been given so much credit for the young woman's turnaround, I ran in alone after her.

She was laying on a hammock, convulsing and sobbing. I instantly commanded the demon to leave her alone and to come out of her. The young woman immediately faced me with a wicked smile on her lips and a demonic spirit flew at me with great force. I was tackled to the ground and unable to get away.

About that time, my husband came looking for me. He had an alert from the Holy Spirit and had left the meeting to find me. Tom discerned what was taking place and immediately commanded the powers of darkness to leave me alone, and he grabbed me up, and got me out of there.

Not only was I very shaken, I was in trouble with Tom for going in alone. We eventually went back into the meeting, but I did not have strength to minister. When we pulled out of the church that night to go back to where we were staying, I felt awful.

One positive outcome was that the shock of what she had done jarred the young woman into repentance. As always, when there is submission to God, the enemy loses and victory is sure. I forgave the young woman and left her, still able to speak and hopefully free.

We flew out the next day and upon arriving home, I still felt terrible, drained and defeated. Eventually, in God's goodness, He showed me the pride that had put me in the path of danger. Because I thought I was an expert with experience and invincible, I was vulnerable to attack. When I repented and confessed my sin to others, I was completely healed — and much wiser!

Now, instead of spontaneously moving, I ask Jesus if He is moving in the direction where I want to hurry to meet a need. If I don't sense His movement, I don't go!

One night I was part of a deliverance session where a woman was saying that she wanted release but was resistant when we tried to pray for her. The other members of the deliverance team had walked out of the sanctuary and were getting ready to leave.

I was gathering up my stuff around the altar when the woman (who was on the other side of the altar) suddenly said to me in a unnaturally low and strange voice, "I can take you down with my little finger!" I continued to gather my stuff and as I walked out, I said, *"Greater is He who is in me than he who is in the world"* (I John 4:4). As I walked out, I looked around and saw that the woman was now pushed back physically by an unseen restraining hand! Jesus had given her opportunity and she had not taken it and it was time for me to safely leave!

Of course I have many stories of complete deliverance and dramatic changes in people as they are freed! Most of the time, if a person will repent, the demon has no more right to them and has to leave.

Be prepared for certain physical demonstrations of freedom. It is not uncommon for a person to vomit as a demon comes out. Other physical responses can happen and you may need to help individuals to not feel embarrassed by what happens.

Cleansing

I teach our Prayer Team Ministers to always wash themselves off after a deliverance session. One of the uses (in Scripture) for anointing oil is cleansing. I instruct our prayers to take some oil and ask God to cleanse them of all repercussions or residue.

Think of it like this: my friend's husband, Bryan, is a police officer. Bryan says that he is glad for the commute home from his job because he has time to clean himself off from all of the evil characters and situations he has dealt with during the day. Bryan says that if he doesn't ask God to cleanse him and wash his mind, he brings the stuff home with him and into his house. He has noticed the reaction in his boys when he doesn't cleanse off the day before he gets home. But when he allows the Lord to wash him (of other people's evil), there is peace in his own household!

After confronting the demonic, we must go to Jesus for rest and refreshing. Recently the Lord called me to lay aside all of my plans and people and COME. He said, "Come, My child, you are weary. Come, you are heavy laden. I will give you rest." As I came to Him, He rested and restored me. He always does!

Five Characteristics of How Jesus Dealt With a Demon

"On the Sabbath [Jesus] entered the synagogue and taught . . . Now there was a man in their synagogue with an unclean spirit. And he cried out, 'Let us alone! What have we to do with You, Jesus of Nazareth? Did You come to destroy us? I know who You are — the Holy One of God!' But Jesus rebuked him, saying, "Be quiet, and come out of him!" And when the unclean spirit had convulsed him and cried out with a loud voice, he came out of him. Then they were all amazed, so that they questioned among themselves, saying, 'What is this? What new doctrine is this? For with authority He commands even the unclean spirits, and they obey Him.' And immediately His fame spread throughout all the region around Galilee"
(Mark 1:21-28).

1. Jesus dealt with the demon, not the man. Jesus expelled the demon from the man. He didn't make the man leave the Synagogue.

2. Jesus wasn't disturbed about dealing with the demon.

3. When the demon began to talk, Jesus told him to be quiet.

4. The man with the demon was a church attendee.

5. The confrontation with the demon spread Jesus' influence.

Notice that the Lord was not troubled either by the demon or the public exorcism. Expelling demons was as normal a part of Jesus' ministry as preaching! And so shall it be of ours, as we go about continuing the work of our Lord Jesus!

Sometimes we feel like we are ineffective because we do not see dramatic or even visible changes when we pray for deliverance. I encourage myself with remembering what Smith Wigglesworth said: "I am not moved by what I see. I am not moved by what I feel. I am moved only by what I believe."

Remember that you cannot control people. God gives all of us freewill and He never overrides this gift. Remember also that it is up to the person to act on their deliverance and healing.

Understand Why People Seemingly Lose Their Healing

When people are in a place where faith is strong and the gifts of the Spirit are moving, it's comparatively easy for them to receive healing. This is what happens in a great church service or other Holy Spirit-led meeting. However, when a person gets back home and is on their own, the devil comes and tries to put symptoms back on them. If a person does not have a foundation of faith in them, the devil puts the same thing back on them. That's the reason why you sometimes see people get delivered, and then the next time you see them they are right back where they started. Why did they seemingly lose their healing? They were probably unprepared for the fight. This is why it is so important for individuals to get connected to a Spirit-filled church where there is a strong atmosphere of faith.

The Good Fight of Faith

A friend of mine, Vivian, fought for five years for her healing. As a child in South Africa, she was diagnosed with Sickle Cell Anemia. Vivian was not expected to live past the age of 18 and was often hospitalized. One evening she attended a great crusade where there was prayer for healing. Vivian knew that God healed her body that night, but she continued to be very sick. Vivian didn't let go of believing that God had indeed healed her. For the next five years, Vivian continued to be in and out of hospitals. Sometimes she was very close to death. But, she continued to believe God and trust in the healing that she knew she had received at the crusade.

One day Vivian woke up in the morning feeling good. The battle was over; her healing was finally manifesting in her body. And the health continued the next day and the next. Today Vivian is a vibrant married woman in her thirties!

Train my hands for war! Teach me to stand and fight back on behalf of Your righteous cause, oh Lord!

Working Hard to Believe

"Our work is to seek the assistance of God; God's work is to accomplish the work. Our work is to acknowledge our helplessness; God's work is to be the Helper. Our work is to be open to God's work in our lives; God's work is to work within and around us to fulfill His purposes." O. Hallesby

There is often a battle in the minds of people who need healing or other ministry. The root of illness often resides in the thought life and the battle to renew the mind is challenging. The enemy attacks the thought life because he knows that anxiety and fear give him ammunition.

When I help people who are working so hard to believe for a miracle, I encourage them that they don't need to do anything but to be still and receive from God. I train our prayer team ministers to let people know that we will believe for them. Not that faith is unimportant! It's just that the effort to believe pushes some people into anxiety.

To relieve the pressure felt by a person who is struggling to believe, tell them, "I have the faith for this one — just be at peace!" And when they let their guard down and don't have to fight to get something — they just may begin to move in true biblical faith!

With faith comes the desire to please God. With this desire, a person can be led to repent and is able to submit to God. Remember that submission to God and resisting the devil dislodges demons.

"Submit to God. Resist the devil and he will flee from you" (James 4:6-8).

"Submit to God, Resist the Devil . . . be clothed with humility, for God resists the proud, But gives grace to the humble" (1 Peter 5:5-6).

A Few Characteristics of Demons:

Derek Prince says this: *"I describe demons as disembodied spirit beings that have an intense craving to occupy physical bodies. Apparently their first choice is a human body; but rather than remain in a disembodied condition, they are willing to enter even the body of an animal (see Luke 8:32-33)."* They Shall Expel Demons

- Demons can make decisions: ***"I will return to my house from which I came"*** (Matthew 12:44).

- A demon can feel: ***"Even the demons believe and tremble"*** (James 2:19).

- Demons can think: ***"I know who You are — the Holy One from God"*** (Mark 1:24).

- Demons are able to speak (as seen in the Scriptures referenced above).

Good People Can Be Carriers of Demons

At a recent service, the enemy was lurking and disrupting as we had at least two people distracting others during worship.

Good people sometimes bring in foul spirits. We must expect to confront and bind the demonic with our individual and collective shields of faith up and large!

Many people assume that "manifesting" means to foam at the mouth and speak in guttural noise — or other preconceived ideas. These things take place sometimes but not usually.

Manifest means to "make known" (emphanidzo; appear, come to view, reveal, exhibit, make visible). The demons that manifest at a service are usually there to cause confusion and resistance.

It is often Christians who are used by the devil to disrupt or distract. Just because someone causing disruption in the worship is a Christian (and may have an impressive resume) does not mean that they cannot be used by Satan in an area of their lives.

Most of us think that a person is either free of demons or full of demons (demon possessed). I am sorry to say that many believers are not free of demons.

Now, before you throw this book away, please read on.

Possession refers to the voluntary reception of a control spirit by a spirit medium; possession implies total ownership. The people who come to services are usually just church people who have some unsurrendered areas in their lives and not people who are full of the devil!

People who come to church may allow a demon to interrupt the worship (or any other aspect of the service) through them. The nature of deception is that we don't know when we are deceived. Hence, the people who cause confusion have no idea that they are not supposed to do whatever it is they are doing (even sitting in resistance affects the atmosphere — See Mark 6:5).

We love people and we want to help them. We want them to come to church and want to protect the other people who are in the meeting! We need to see clearly, get rid of former ideas, and let God grow us up.

What Do We Do?

So, the question is, what do we do when we perceive that a person is allowing the devil to use them to disrupt and distract other people from what God wants to do?

Most all of us have been in a setting where something took place that just did not feel right. If you have been around a revival meeting or other place of ministry where people are getting freed, you may have seen and heard some unusual things.

I remember when I first heard about holy laughter. A friend told me how she had been to a meeting where God was moving in such a powerful way through joy and people were laughing for extended periods of time — loudly! I had never seen or heard of such a thing. It wasn't long after that I attended a meeting where this happened. The atmosphere was beautiful as individuals were receiving breakthrough joy from God.

But, then, as this kind of move of God began to happen more frequently, the atmosphere didn't feel the same. Some people were jumping on the band-wagon to be in on the "in thing."

Instead of enjoying God's presence, sometimes the meetings would feel out of order, disjointed and frustrating. What did I discern? Mixture. Wherever there are people, a mixture of different spirits may be present.

Train Your Senses to Discern

The Word of God teaches that we are to train our senses to discern between good and evil. We must not be unaware of the things pertaining to the spirit realm or we may be taken advantage of.

Hebrews 5:14 states:
"Solid food belongs to those who are of full age, that is, those who by reason of use have their senses exercised to discern both good and evil."
"Those whose senses and mental faculties are trained by practice to discriminate and distinguish . . ." (Amplified Bible).
"Because of the use are having the senses exercised . . ." (Young).

Most people have not yet utilized their full potential for wisdom because of an inability to hear, see and perceive the movement of the Great Unseen God.

How did Jesus stay tuned in — at all times — to what His Father in Heaven was saying and doing? For one thing, He paid close attention. If you have read any of the stories about the Aborigine tribes of Australia, you may have learned that this people group has an astonishing ability to smell! The ability to smell is a matter of survival. Having trained this sense for centuries, some of these people can actually pick up the scent of an animal that is miles away or of a human who was in the area hours before!

While a few people may have a dramatically better sense of smell, most of us probably just don't pay attention.

We must learn to recognize God's nearness, to hear the voice of Him who rarely speaks audibly and observe the actions of Him who is invisible; be so in tune with God that we know where He is moving and where the human spirit (or the devil) is moving. Our senses (smell, taste, touch, hearing and sight) must be trained.

At a recent service, a woman began to laugh during worship in a most unusual way. Prior to her outburst, the Spirit of God had been moving in a wonderful way. Possibly she felt the presence of the Lord and was blessed into joy and laughter. But her continued eruption began to bring disruption. Most eyes turned to her and the atmosphere changed to confusion and bewilderment. (This was not a quiet, somber meeting prior to the woman's loud laughter. The meeting had been full of shouts of joy, and boisterous singing!) At times like this, it is difficult to discern what to do. I waited on God, asking Him to show me what He wanted. He impressed on me that the woman was drawing attention to herself on purpose. She had the grace to employ self-control (a fruit of the Spirit, Galatians 5), but she wanted to be known as a Spirit-filled person and be valued as such. Motive is the intention of the heart and can be discerned by those who have trained their senses. The fact was, the episode just didn't *feel right.*

What did we do? I sent two of our prayer team ministers to stand by the woman. They gently came behind and beside her, commanding a dramatic spirit to be silent. As they did so, the woman came into alignment with God's Spirit. Had she not, the prayer team ministers would have quietly talked with her and asked her a couple of questions to help her discern her motives. If she would not have respected their authority, they would have invited her into one of our prayer rooms where there could be loving ministry.

If this seems a bit controlling to you, perhaps you have not been in this healthy of an atmosphere! A person who is manifesting another spirit needs help. To withhold from a person the help that is needed because we are not sure what spirit the person is of, is unkind! We must have trained senses!

"In these last days, God is marshaling prayer warriors who are anointed to gain jurisdictional authority over the powers of darkness so that families, communities, governments, ministries, corporations, countries, kingdoms and nations are brought back into divine alignment, and individuals fulfill purpose and maximize their personal potential."
Dr. N. Cindy Trimm

In his book, Learning to Interpret the Flow With the Spirit of God, Kenneth Hagin states, " *In the twenty-eighth verse of First Corinthians 14, there's a twofold meaning here, whether you realize it or not. 'But if there be no INTERPRETER, let him keep silence in the church; and let him speak to himself, and to God.' Notice Paul didn't say, "If there's no one present who can interpret." He didn't say, "If there is no one present with the interpretation of tongues." He said, "If there be no INTERPRETER. . . ."*

I believe that the Lord wants His people to be able to interpret what He is doing and where He is moving; as stated previously, to be able to sense what God wants. I think there is a great deal more to "interpretation" than what we have yet seen.

Be Prepared to Pray for People in Need

I encourage our Prayer Ministers to always be ready to pray for people, no matter where they are! Part of being ready is to do the following things:

- Put on the armor of God daily (Ephesians 6)

- Pray in the Name of Jesus — Remember and believe that Jesus' name is all powerful (Mark 16:17-18)

- Memorize Scripture

- Use the Word of God as your sword. God's Word flashes light

- God's Word is the Truth that sets people free (John 8:32)

- Proclaim the Blood of Jesus Christ

- The Blood is what covers sin. Never be ashamed of the Cross of Christ Jesus — it is at the Cross of suffering that the enemy was defeated (Colossians 2:15)

- Celebrate the Lord's Supper often (I Corinthians 11:26)

- Pray with fasting (Acts 14:23)

- Walk in the Spirit (Galatians 5)

- Spend time daily in worship and praise (Psalm 150)

- And, one more (surprising) thing: eat meat

The Holy Spirit gave me revelation about eating meat to prepare for spiritual battle through the book, "He Came To Set The Captives Free" by Rebecca Brown, MD (pages 184-187). I recommend research into the importance of protein in the diet in regard to spiritual warfare.

"If we look at the various spiritual warriors of renown in the Old Testament, we will find that every time, before they engaged

in a great battle, God prepared them with the eating of meat."
Dr. Rebecca Brown

The entire subject of demons is not pleasant and no one enjoys fighting with these evil spirits. But the light and freedom that is evident on the face of one who has been delivered is priceless. It is love for God, a desire to do what He said to do and the compassion for people that compels us to deal with demons.

Questions

1. When have you tried to cast out a demon and felt that you failed?

2. Has there been a time when you walked into a situation where God was not at work and you got into trouble?

   What happened?

3. When have you seen God move in powerful deliverance, setting a person free from demonic oppression?

4. Do you believe that God wants to use your life to bring freedom into the lives of those oppressed by demons?

5. What is the sequence, as found in James 4:7, that causes a demon to flee?

For You to Pray:

O Lover of my soul, I commit all things to You; I will not fear, for You are with me. I relax in the unknown of anything that You will call me to do. I am at rest with the unknown of You and of Your ways, for what I do know — You are Love, You are good, You love me — is plenty and enough to carry me all the days of my life! Use me to help others, O God, that they might come into the fullness of Your love!

Chapter 11

Keys in Your Hand

Come to Jesus so that your heart is aligned with the love of God, coming to embrace Him who is reaching to embrace you. Then go — for the sake of those who are still bound, and for the world that God loves.

Now that you know the great authority that you have in Jesus, you have the double portion that you acquired through praying for others; you have banked the power stored up through the discipline of fasting; and you are submitted and willing to deal with the demonic; get ready to leap forward in faith! There are people who need your help right now. You can set captives free with your loving words of truth, in the name of Jesus.

Setting the Bound Free!

Many times a person will come forward after a service for prayer and I will discern that they are held captive by "feelings" or attitudes that they can't seem to shake. Depression, anger, fear, confusion, condemnation and weariness are common issues. Feelings of hopelessness are common as people admit to believing that "there is no remedy for my problem".

Understanding the root cause of a problem will give you insight into how to help yourself or another person.

Our Lord, Jesus Christ, announced that He came to proclaim liberty to the captives.

> *The Spirit of the Lord GOD is*
> *upon Me, Because the LORD has*
> *anointed Me To preach good tidings*
> *to the poor; He has sent Me to heal*
> *the brokenhearted, To proclaim liberty*
> *to the <u>captives</u>, And the opening of*
> *the prison to those who are bound"*
> (Isaiah 61:1).

A Captive

Let's look at the definition of captive: *To be held or taken prisoner.* The Lord said that people who are held captive can have liberty or freedom proclaimed to them. In other words, you can pray (proclaim freedom) for captives, and if they will receive their freedom by faith, they will be set free. You can often see the change in a person's face immediately.

A Prisoner

One who is confined in prison is a "harder case." Those in prison must have an opening of the prison doors before they can come out. What are these prison doors and how does a person get put in a spiritual jail?

> *[Jesus Christ said], "Be reconciled to your brother, and then*
> *come and offer your gift. Agree with your adversary quickly,*
> *while you are on the way with him, lest your adversary deliver*
> *you to the judge, the judge hand you over to the officer, and you be*
> *thrown into prison"* (Matthew 5:24-25).

I have found that prisoners are usually locked up because of an unwillingness to forgive. The door that needs to swing open is forgiveness.

I love to pray for children because they are usually freed easily from whatever is bothering them. One day I was asked to pray for a young girl who had been having headaches and needed healing. As I prayed for her, I felt her resistance to healing. he was holding onto the headache. I prayed for healing again and then asked her if her head felt better. She shook her head and continued to look downcast. I prayed for her again and then asked her again if she felt better. Again she said that she did not.

As I looked over to the child's mother, I was impressed by the Holy Spirit to ask her if she had been giving her daughter the time that she needed. The mother admitted that she had been too busy lately, and had not spent time listening to or paying attention to her daughter. I asked the mother if she would like to tell the Lord that she was sorry for neglecting her child.

After she did so, I asked her to tell her daughter that she was sorry. When she did, the little girl thought for a moment, and then decided to forgive her mother. After she forgave, I was able to pray for the child and she was healed. I then bound a spirit of self-pity from bothering the child.

This is a simple case of being locked up because of offense and lack of forgiveness. The root issue was addressed and hopefully the mother gained wisdom through this incident that has continued to bring needed change.

Once again, discernment is needed as you pray for people. You may need to ask if there is someone that the individual needs to forgive. The one that needs to be forgiven may be another person, it may be themselves, or it could be God. The most important thing that needs to take place is for the person to come into agreement with God's way. He always forgives, and in order for the individual to be set free, they must agree with God's command to forgive.

If a person is unwilling to forgive, you cannot violate God's Word and bring that person out of prison. Please read the following phrase and the corresponding Scripture:

Binding and loosing on Earth is coming into agreement with what is said and done in Heaven.

"Truly I tell you, whatever you forbid and declare to be improper and unlawful on earth must be what is already forbidden in heaven, and whatever you permit and declare proper and lawful on earth must be what is already permitted in heaven" (Matthew 16:19). Amplified Bible

You Can Only Loose What God Has Loosed.

When Jesus Christ said, *"Woman, you are loosed from your infirmity"* (Luke 13:12), He was speaking of something that was taking place in Heaven. Why? Because the woman was ready for a move of God! People who hold onto their own selfish ways are not ready for God to help them. This is often because they will not forgive. Refusing to obey God's Word is a lack of submission and, ultimately, rebellion against God.

A couple of years ago, Tom and I listened to an evangelist from Mexico who was speaking at The City Church in Seattle, Washington. This evangelist told the story of a man who was in his 70s and who had been blind for 36 years. The man attended a healing meeting held by the evangelist and had come forward for prayer. As the evangelist began praying for him, he was impressed by the Holy Spirit to ask the man if there was someone that he had not forgiven 36 years before. The man then confessed that his wife had left him 36 years earlier, and that he had never forgiven her. The evangelist asked him if he was ready to forgive her — the man answered, "Yes." When he submitted to God, asked for forgiveness and announced he had forgiven his wife, the evangelist prayed and immediately the man received his sight!

"Forgive, and you will be forgiven" (Luke 6:37).

"If you do not forgive men their trespasses, neither will your Father forgive your trespasses" (Matthew 6:15).

"If you have anything against anyone, forgive him, that your Father in heaven may also forgive you your trespasses. But if you do not forgive, neither will your Father in heaven forgive your trespasses" (Mark 11:25-26).

Praying Again

When you pray for an individual, don't be afraid to ask them if they feel better or if God touched them. Sometimes a person may feel obligated to tell you that they are better when they are not. You can ask an additional question, "What did God do for you?" If there is still a need or if they have not felt the touch of God, you may need to pray again. The Lord Jesus Christ modeled this in the following Scripture about the blind man:

> *"Then [Jesus Christ] came to Bethsaida; and*
> *they brought a blind man to Him, and begged Him to touch*
> *him. So He took the blind man by the hand and led him out*
> *of the town. And when He had spit on his eyes and put His hands*
> *on him, He asked him if he saw anything. And he looked up and*
> *said, " I see men like trees, walking." Then He put His hands*
> *on his eyes <u>again</u> and made him look up. And he was restored*
> *and saw everyone clearly"* (Mark 8:22-25).

Remember, it is God who does the healing and saving. We simply must be attentive to what He wants to do. If He wants you to pray again, don't let your own fear or paradigms get in the way!

Commanding Demons to Go to the Cross

Prayer Team Ministers at Horizon are taught to send demons to the Cross of Jesus Christ. At the Cross, the powers of darkness were and are completely disarmed! In other words, their weapons are taken away from them and they are rendered completely powerless to inflict harm any longer. In fact, the principalities and powers of darkness were (and are) made a public (out-in-the-open) spectacle (display) of powerlessness at the Cross, as Jesus Christ triumphs over them!

> *"Having disarmed principalities and powers, He*
> *[Jesus Christ] made a public spectacle of them,*
> *triumphing over them in it [the cross]"* (Colossians 2:15).

A few years ago I had an experience that woke me up to the importance of paying attention when casting demons out of people.

I attended a conference at a large church in the northwest where there was a special speaker who talked on prayer. After she spoke, she invited anyone who was suffering with depression to come to the front and be delivered. Many people lined the front of the church as the speaker began to minister deliverance from depression. As she began to move through the people, she came to the fourth person waiting and began to forcefully command the demon of depression to leave. I immediately saw a demon leave the person's body but, to my horror, it then went searching over and through the crowd of people in the congregation for a place to go.

I was appalled as 'it' found an accessible person and 'dove into' her. I had no idea that this could happen and was stunned. I began to cry out to God for protection over the unsuspecting crowd.

Eventually I approached the speaker (who was still carelessly casting out demons) and tried to make her understand what had transpired. She brushed me off and continued her "ministry".

Later, I spent time repenting of all the times that I have carelessly done the same kind of thing. I asked the Holy Spirit for wisdom and instruction as to where to send the demons. He gave me Colossians 2:15, and spoke to my heart that the demons would be disarmed at the Cross and unable to harm bystanders. This experience actually changed the way I minister and how I instruct others to minister. Casting out demons takes great wisdom and insight from God's Word.

I had a similar experience recently. I was ministering in a line of pastors (we, the pastors, lined up facing each other and the people in the meeting were invited to walk through and be prayed for). Several times I watched as demons were told to go out of a person, as the person was coming through the prayer line. I watched as the demons came up and hovered over a person for a moment, before reentering. Why?

Do you remember when Jesus sent a legion of demons into pigs (Matthew 8:30)? The Word says that the demons begged Jesus to let them go into a herd of swine that were feeding close by. Where would they have gone if Jesus had not sent them into the pigs? In Matthew 12:43, Jesus states, *"When an unclean spirit goes out of a man, he goes through dry places, seeking rest, and finds none. Then he says, 'I will return to my house from which I came.'"*

From this Scripture we learn that demons want to get back into the person from whom they were cast out. Our task is to help the person who is being delivered continue to be free, even after they leave the time of personal ministry.

Maybe this simple picture will help. Most of us have seen a western or cowboy movie. In this kind of story, the bad guy usually has a gun (is "armed"). The sheriff comes looking for the bad guy and when he finds him, tells him to give up his gun. Sometimes the bad guy resists and then the sheriff cocks his gun. This scares the bad guy into handing over his gun. He is now "disarmed".

At the Cross, the powers of darkness were and are completely disarmed! In other words, their weapons are taken away from them and they are rendered powerless to inflict hurt any longer. We have authority to proclaim their disarmament at the Cross and it is there that we enforce the deliverance that Jesus paid for!

God Wants People Free

Who did Jesus give the keys of freedom to? YOU! You can help to unlock chains and watch people who were once bound move into blessing. In the name of Jesus, help people repent of their sins and then get free of the bondages that sin caused. People are in need of a word of courage! They have wayward kids, health problems, financial issues and weariness. You have the answer: Jesus!

Listening for Clues

As you listen to the words that a person speaks, you will find that there are clues to what's going on in the heart.

Jesus said, "For out of the abundance of the
heart his mouth speaks" (Luke 6:45).

Read through the following examples and be empowered as you familiarize yourself with the issues and solutions from the Word of God:

Confusion — may be a *Priority* Issue

You hear the person with the need say, "I feel so confused."
The person who makes a statement about feeling confused is probably not spending time meditating on God's Word.

Ask these questions:

"Are you making time to read God's Word?"
"Are you taking time for daily prayer?"
"Are you making worship a priority?"

"For where envy and self-seeking exist, confusion and
every evil thing are there" (James 3:16).

"Seek first the kingdom" (Matthew 6:33).

Help the person repent of putting other things above God. Then tell "confusion" to go and to be bound at the Cross of Jesus Christ! Then ask Father to (loose) pour in His peace.

Depression — may be an <u>Anxiety Issue</u> (see Proverbs 12:25)

You hear the words, "I feel so down" or "I am depressed."
The person who is depressed has probably been worrying about something.

Ask this question:
"Is there something that you are worried about (finances, future, family)?"

> *"Anxiety in the heart of man causes depression"*
> (Proverbs 12:25).

> *"Therefore I say to you, do not*
> *worry about your life . . ."* (Matthew 6:25-31).

Help the person repent for giving place to worry. Help him put his trust in God. Then tell "worry" to leave the person and be bound at the Cross of Jesus Christ. Ask the Holy Spirit to come and (loose) bring rest and trust into the person's soul.

> *"Submit to God. Resist the devil and he will*
> *flee from you"* (James 4:7).

Our task is to help individuals repent (this is submitting to God), turn from their sin (resist the devil), and then to tell the demon to go to the Cross (he will flee)!

Unbelief — may be a <u>People Pleasing Issue</u>

You hear the words, "God seems so far away."
The person may be looking for affirmation and strokes from other people instead of paying attention to what God says about him.

Ask this question:
"Is there someone you are trying to please or gain approval from?"

> *"How can you believe, who receive honor from*
> *one another, and do not seek the honor that comes*
> *from the only God"* (John 5:44)?

> *"The fear of man brings a snare, But whoever trusts*
> *in the LORD shall be safe"* (Proverbs 29:25).

Encourage the person that you are helping, to turn their eyes upon Jesus Christ. Remind them that He is the most important Person. Help them to repent of putting their hope in people instead of in God. After they repent, tell the "fear of man" to leave, in the name of Jesus, and be bound at the Cross. Loose the love of God, which casts out all fear (I John 4:18).

"Be of good cheer, daughter; your faith has made you well"
(Matthew 9:22).

"According to your faith let it be to you" (Matthew 9:29).

"Great is your faith! Let it be to you as you desire" (Matthew 15:28).

"Your faith has made you . . . healed of your affliction" (Mark 5:34).

"Go your way; your faith has made you well" (Mark 10:52).

"Your faith has saved you. Go in peace" (Luke 7:50).

"Arise, go your way. Your faith has made you well" (Luke 17:19).

"Receive your sight; your faith has made you well" (Luke 18:42).

Jesus Christ

Fear — may be a Love Receiver Issue

You hear the person say, "I just don't feel worthy of God's love."

Ask these questions:
"Are you able to sleep at night?"
"Do you feel afraid about anything right now?"

"There is no fear in love; but perfect love casts out fear,
because fear involves torment. But he who fears has
not been made perfect in love. We love Him because He
first loved us" (I John 4:18-19)

Encourage the person to express their love to God out loud. Have them simply say, "I love you, Lord Jesus." Then encourage the person to thank God for loving them. If the individual is not willing to acknowledge God's love for them personally, use John 3:16 and ask them to come into agreement with God's love for every individual, including them. (If they refuse, you may need to recommend some counseling and move on.) After the person has loved the Lord verbally and acknowledged His love for them, tell the spirit of fear to leave, in the name of Jesus Christ. Use II Timothy 1:7: *"For God has not given us a spirit of fear, but of power and of love and of a sound mind."*

Bind the spirit of fear at the Cross and command it to return no more! (You may also recommend that the person purchase the book, "Freedom From Fear" which is available on our website — www.hiswaytoday.org)

Anger — may be a Lack of Forgiveness Issue

You pick up on the words spoken, "I feel frustrated."

Ask these questions:
"Is there someone that has offended you?"
"Are you angry with yourself for any reason?"
"Has God let you down?"

> *"And this I pray, that your love may abound still more and more in knowledge and all discernment, that you may approve the things that are excellent, that you may be sincere and without offense till the day of Christ, being filled with the fruits of righteousness which are by Jesus Christ, to the glory and praise of God"* (Philippians 1:9-11).

> *"Be angry, and do not sin, do not let the sun go down on your wrath, nor give place to the devil"* (Ephesians 4:26-27).

Lead the person to forgive whoever they are holding resentment toward. As they repent, you can command "frustration" to leave them. You may also encourage them to repent of anger. As they repent, command an angry spirit to be bound at the Cross of Jesus Christ. Ask the Holy Spirit to pour in (loose) His grace into the person.

Weariness — may be a Hopelessness Issue

The person you are praying with says, "I am so tired."

Ask this question:
"Is there someone or something that has disappointed you?"

> *"And let us not grow weary while doing good, for in due season we shall reap if we do not lose heart"* (Galatians 6:9).

Help the person repent of giving place to irritation and impatience. Encourage them to submit to the Word of God and believe that God is at work. After they have submitted to God, tell disappointment to be bound at the Cross of Jesus Christ. Command hopelessness to leave them alone and return no more. Bind the hopelessness at the Cross. Bind weariness and remind the person that the joy of the Lord is their strength. Ask the Holy Spirit to (loose) pour in joy!

Condemnation — May be a Pride Issue

You hear the person say, "I feel like I can't do anything right" or "I feel guilty all the time."

Ask these questions:
"Do you feel that you should be further along in your life than you are?" "Does it seem like other people have better things happen to them than you do?"

> *"Agree with your adversary quickly, while you are on the way with him, lest your adversary deliver you to the judge, the judge hand you over to the officer, and you be thrown into prison"* (Matthew 5:25).

> *"There is now no condemnation for those who are in Christ Jesus"* (Romans 8:1).

Lead the person to give God permission to do whatever He wants to do in their life. Lead them to repent of wanting to control their own life instead of letting God have complete control. Encourage them to repent of pride. After there is true submission to God's way, bind "condemnation" at the Cross of Jesus Christ and return no more! Ask the Holy Spirit to (loose) pour in His grace.

Binding and Loosing Really Works

You may wonder if your words have any real power to affect change. Jesus said that if you have faith the size of a tiny mustard seed, you can move mountains (Matthew 17:20). Believing what Jesus said is an act of faith. The prayers that you pray for individuals, you pray by faith.

What will happen as you step out in faithful ministry to people is that you will see some individuals healed and delivered! The more miracles you experience, the more your faith will increase.

Questions

1. What does it mean to be bound in prison?

2. What is the difference between being in prison and being held captive?

3. When have you prayed for someone to be loosed from bondage and seen immediate change?

4. Has there been a time when you have prayed for someone and the person has remained bound? Do you have insight as to the reason?

5. Is there something that you need to repent of right now? Ask God to search your heart.

For You To Pray:

Search me, O God! Please show me if there is any unforgiveness in me toward anyone. I invite You to bring up anything from which You want to deliver me. I will repent and I will forgive. Please help me, O God, and please free me from all captivity and any jail that You alone see. Thank You that You will!

Chapter 12

PER-SONIC POWER

Discernment in Speaking Words of Wisdom and Prophecy

"But if they are prophets, and if the word of the LORD
is with them, let them now make intercession to the
LORD of hosts . . ." (Jeremiah 27:18).

People who value true prayer know that they do not merely speak into thin air; their words carry weight and have power. Consider the way in which God formed the world — He spoke and it became! Genesis 1:3: *"Then God said, "'Let there be light'; and there was light."*

Likewise, as those created in the image of God, we have the gift of speech and the possibility of creating with our words.

With our words, we can advance the Kingdom of God! What a great privilege and what a big responsibility.

Words

Words have great power. Right now, as you read the next paragraph on this page, you may have a chemical reaction in your physical body from the words. Are you ready?

Let's think about warm, chewy, just-baked brownies coming out of the oven. Oh, they smell so good! Can you smell them?

They will taste so delicious as they melt in your mouth — especially with vanilla ice cream melting all over the chocolate brownie! Is your mouth watering yet? Reading words on a page can actually cause a response in your physical body.

How would you like to speak words that would make everyone around you hungry for God?

I believe that having the right message at the right hour releases a realm of supernatural activity that will draw the people around you to God!

Not being athletic, I never experienced the feeling of being cheered on by spectators during a sporting event. It wasn't until I was in my forties, wanting to get some exercise by attempting to run on a school track, that I felt the exhilaration and propulsion of spurring-forward words. As I was completing my second lap (and wanting to quit), my husband, began to jog behind me, shouting words of encouragement, "You can do it; keep going; you are doing great; looking good; don't give up; keep those feet moving; you can do it . . ." With newfound strength and endurance, I pressed on, catapulted forward by WORDS!

In the same way, your words can encourage and strengthen other people and help to propel them forward into blessing. Conversely, your words can also bring destruction.

Everyone has been hurt by words spoken to them (or about them) in their life. The Bible states that *"death and life are in the power of the tongue"* (Proverbs 18:21). As you minister to people, you do not want to speak any words to any person that could bring harm. It is of the utmost importance that we learn to listen to God and *"be swift to hear and slow to speak"* (James 1:19).

Slow to Speak

If you are a person who serves (or desires to serve) in a ministry, know that ministry is a place of authority. You have been entrusted with a gift to help other people and you must be careful with what you say. As you are trustworthy with your mouth, God will reveal secret things to you. The Lord invites us, *"Call to Me, and I will answer you, and show you great and mighty things, which you do not know"* (Jeremiah 33:3).

As the Holy Spirit shows us the hidden things, we must be wise! We do not need to speak everything that the Lord shows us as we pray. Jesus Christ knew all kinds of things about people that He did not confront or say out loud. He saw clearly into people's lives! Neither should we say everything we are shown by the Holy Spirit about a person. We must know what God wants spoken.

"Our souls, wrought with insecurities, are highly sensitive to the criticisms and compliments of others. In the search to find oneself, such words are poured into young hearts like molten steel which, as they cool, are fused into our natures. How many of today's adults believe they are mentally slow simply because, as children, they absorbed into their self-contempt the negative, thoughtless scolding of a teacher or parent." Frances Frangipane, The Three Battlegrounds, page 30

Create Hope With Your Words!

We are all persons and the meaning of this word is accurate because *person* means: one who sound comes through! "Per" means passing through and "son" sonic, sound! Speech and language is an amazing gift and distinguishes us as the only creature made in God's image. He spoke and like Him, we speak.

We talk, and what we say creates and releases a reality that invites people to move forward with God. Therefore, we must guard our hearts and train ourselves to declare the right words. Our words can actually set a condition or climate that will draw people into their destiny!

I spoke on this very thing in church recently (from Isaiah 35), **"A highway shall be here—and it shall be called the Highway of Holiness."** I believe that when masses of people step up into position with the right message and live in purity, there is a power released that is exponential in effect!

Can you imagine the force of the breakthrough prayers as each of us walk (run) in wisdom and purity?

A Highway of Holiness! A highway is a place of easy access. Your holy mouth can actually give those, who don't know Christ, a road to know Him!

"Run among the people and look for anyone who is faltering . . . let them know that this is no time to falter — this is their moment" (Isaiah 35:3-4).

We ARE in the middle of a divine moment! You can spur others on in Christ as you give the right message. Take the Scriptures about the Good News message to heart and then find anyone who is afraid and tell them: "Don't be afraid, God is for you!" Your vocal chords are the supreme instrument for releasing God's purposes into reality!

Discernment

What happens when you walk among people with the right message, declaring the word of what God is going to do? It actually attracts God into the situation to do what was declared He would do! What a gift and what a responsibility God has given to each of us! How can we fulfill all that He wants accomplished?

Let the Prophets Intercede

God's Word states, *"Let the prophets intercede"* (Jeremiah 27:18). Many churches have been damaged due to people who have given words of prophecy without the spiritual maturity of knowing when to pray and when to prophesy.

If you want to function in the gift of prophecy, it is vital that you first pray diligently behind the scenes for the person, church or ministry for whom you have received a word! Please be slow to speak!

> *"For we know in part and we prophesy in part.*
> *But when that which is perfect has come,*
> *then that which is in part will be done away"*
> (I Corinthians 13:9).

Trouble in the Church

In one our previous churches we had a woman, Gail*, who operated in the gift of prophecy. But she did not yet understand when to be quiet and when to speak. Gail's husband was a leader in the church, and the family was well respected.

One evening we got a phone call from another prominent family in the church that was very upset by a word they had received from Gail. She had given them a harsh word about the potential death of their child if they didn't do what Gail, the "prophet", believed God was telling them to do through her. And it was not a simple matter of parenting: it was a word about giving their child up for adoption!

*Name Changed

Tom and I tried to mediate between the two families and tried to help Gail back down with her words of judgment, but she refused. She also began to gather support from other church members for her cause.

The family who had received the severe word began to share their grievance with others in the church and gather sympathy. Before we knew it, we had a church split. The two families were now in a feud and taking the church apart through it. The enemy was using both sides to bring destruction.

This was a very painful time for us as we lost many church members and friends. All because one woman who believed she had a word from God could not wait on Him and pray.

"For you can all prophesy one by one, that all may learn and all may be encouraged. And the spirits of the prophets are subject to the prophets. For God is not the author of confusion but of peace, as in all the churches of the saints"
(I Corinthians 14:31-33).

How Can We Know?

How can you know for sure that the Lord wants you to give someone a Word from Him? Through intercession. As we stand before Father God on behalf of another person, we will gain His compassion, His plan and His love. We hear God's voice and we speak what He wants spoken. You must be able to hear God's voice in order to echo what He is saying.

As I train people for ministry, I welcome them to pray for people. But the gift of prophecy requires greater accountability. To operate in the gift of prophecy means that the intense spiritual work required is fulfilled.

When the Apostle Paul encouraged all people to seek the gift of prophecy (I Corinthians 14:39), he was encouraging time and complete devotion to God. He knew that true prophecy requires intense spiritual work and continually propelled people toward full devotion to God. Therefore, at our church, prayer team ministers are welcome to bless people, encourage (exhort) and affirm God's written Word to them. However, to give any words of reproof, confrontation or advice "from God", a person needs to show themselves approved.

*"For the kingdom of God is not eating and drinking,
but righteousness and peace and joy in the Holy Spirit.
For he who serves Christ in these things is acceptable
to God and approved by men"* (Romans 14:17-18).

*"For not he who commends himself is approved, but
whom the Lord commends"* (II Corinthians 10:18).

*"But as we have been approved by God to be entrusted
with the gospel, even so we speak, not as pleasing men,
but God who tests our hearts. For neither at any time did we
use flattering words, as you know, nor a cloak for covetousness —
God is witness. Nor did we seek glory from men, either from you or
from others, when we might have made demands as apostles
of Christ. But we were gentle among you, just as a
nursing mother cherishes her own children"*
(I Thessalonians 2:4-7).

Approval in ministry comes with service and the building of trust. As you minister and the reports come in of help given, love extended and support felt, a greater sphere of influence will be opened for you.

Wait on the Lord and let Him raise you up as you are trustworthy. You really do not want to bring harm.

*"Be diligent to present yourself approved to God, a
worker who does not need to be ashamed, rightly
dividing the word of truth"* (II Timothy 2:15).

Wisdom Gained

When Tom and I were ministering in one of our past churches, I began to operate (more than previously) in the prophetic. As I spent time in the Word and prayer, I was able to see more clearly. But I didn't yet know when to speak and when to keep silent. I remember one specific Sunday when I was praying with a woman after church. I "saw" a demonic spirit on her. As I told her what I saw, she became very angry and shouted at me, "How dare you accuse me of being demon possessed." I tried to assure her that she was not possessed and that we could pray and she could be free of the oppression. This made her even angrier.

Eventually she went to the Elder's Board of our church and I was reprimanded.

In this specific incident, it would have been better if I had closed my mouth and prayed for her at home. She was not ready to hear "everything I knew" in the Spirit. This woman caused much distress in the church body as she complained to many people about me. Ultimately, it was my fault because I was not wise and had cast my *"pearls before swine"* (Matthew 7:6). This incident taught me a much needed lesson in closing my mouth until I pray, listen and get God's mandate!

"Do not give what is holy to the dogs; nor cast your pearls before swine, lest they trample them under their feet, and turn and tear you in pieces" (Matthew 7:6).

At Horizon Christian Church, we are not rigid with rules, but we do offer important guidelines to help protect the church. The following is a list of priorities for the giving of prophecy.

Please follow these prerequisites for the giving of a prophetic word at a public service:

- Those with the gift of prophecy *must be* in active intercession for the work of God in this specific church before proclaiming a prophecy. *"If they are prophets, and if the word of the LORD is with them, let them now make intercession to the LORD of hosts . . ."* (Jeremiah 27:18).

- The word *must be* tested and confirmed by the elders. *"The spirits of the prophets are subject to the prophets"* (I Corinthians 14:32).

- The word *must be* something that could not be known unless the Holy Spirit is speaking it. The woman at the well said to Jesus, *"Sir, I perceive that You are a prophet."* (Then she said to others) "Come, see a Man who told me all things that I ever did" (John 4:19, 29).

- The prophet must complete the Prayer Team Training classes offered through Horizon or His Way. *"Be diligent to present yourself approved to God, a worker who does not need to be ashamed, rightly dividing the word of truth"* (II Timothy 2:15).

There may be exceptions to these qualifications based on the discernment of the elders and as the Holy Spirit leads.

Idle Words

The Bible is filled with wisdom about when to speak and when to keep silent. Jesus was very clear in His instruction about our words when He warned us about idle words in Matthew 12:36-37: ***"I say to you that for every idle word men may speak, they will give account of it in the day of judgment. For by your words you will be justified, and by your words you will be condemned."***

What are idle words? Derek Prince gives a good explanation in his book, They Shall Expel Demons: *"What are idle words? They are words we utter thoughtlessly, words that do not express our real thoughts or intentions. When we are called in question concerning such words, we often excuse ourselves by saying, "I didn't mean it," or "I was only joking," as though this releases us from responsibility. Yet it is precisely these idle words that Jesus warns us against. The fact that many Christians are habitually guilty of speaking idle words does not make it less serious. In fact, anyone who considers this warning of Jesus as unimportant needs to repent. Idle words can open the door to demons. In a fit of exasperation a person may say, "I'm sick and tired" of whatever it may be. He does not mean it literally, but he may be opening the door to a demon of sickness or tiredness. Words concerning death are particularly dangerous. Many times people say, 'I nearly died laughing,' or, 'You'll die when you hear this one!' Death is a dark, evil power, and we are foolish to treat it so lightly. A person might say, "I wish I were dead" or "I'd be better off dead."* These are an invitation to the spirit of death." Derek Prince, They Shall Expel Demons, page 110

Words have spirit-power and it is very important that we watch what we say!

Women Silent in the Church

Several years ago Tom and I were asked be speakers and to team teach as speakers at a pastor's conference. Imagine my concern when we arrived and found a conference center full of all male pastors! There was not a single female in the house — except for me!

Immediately I wanted to give Tom the full responsibility and back out of any teaching. We decided that Tom would take the first session and then I would give it a try after he gave me "clout" as a woman.

Tom gave a great message on leadership and after a break, it was my turn. I found many of the men doing the same thing that had happened in church services, refusing to look at me. They would become engaged at points in the message and their body language would begin to show interest . . . until I looked their way. Then they would look down again, avoiding any kind of affirmative posture.

As Tom and I reflected on the first day of this four-day conference, I was once again ready to throw in the towel. But I knew God had put an important message on my heart about prayer that was potentially life changing, and I had to give it. Again the next day, Tom went first and had a great session. After the break, I stood to give the message on prayer. But before I began, I quoted one Scripture to that conference center full of men, *"Let your women be silent in the church"* (I Corinthians 14:34).

Suddenly, every eye in the building was on me. Then I proceeded to ask a simple question, "How many of you have been hurt by what women have spoken in your church?" Almost every hand in the room shot up. Then I said, "As a woman, I want to stand in the place of those who have hurt you and ask your forgiveness." You could have heard a pin drop. I then went on to explain that the Apostle Paul had warned the women to be silent in the church because of their powerful influence. Paul knew that women who had not yet learned silence and submission were dangerous. I explained that I had also hurt a pastor (in the past) with my tongue and how sorry I was. I hadn't realized my influence. Then I illustrated how the women in their churches could be a great help to the ministry as they are trained, equipped, and blessed. Every ear listened as I explained the role of prayer in building a great church, filled with both men and women of prayer. The session was incredible as healing and anointing came. The rest of the conference was filled with breakthrough!

May we all, both male and female, learn to use our words to build God's Kingdom and bring life to the people whom God loves!

Questions

1. When have you given someone a word of discernment and had it cause trouble?

2. Has someone given you a "word from God" that was not full of mercy and truth?

3. How do you know when God is speaking to you?

4. In your own life, what has the "intense spiritual work" been that has enabled you to be ready to speak for God?

5. What spiritual gifts do you most desire?

6. How would you like those in authority over you to pray specifically for you?

For You to Pray:

Father, I ask that You set a guard over my mouth that I might not bring any harm with my words. Please help me to pay attention to Your check and to alter my speech according to Your prompting. Then, O God, use my mouth to bring hope and healing to people! Forgive me for when I have brought harm and please help me to never do it again. In Jesus' name!

Chapter 13

Boldly and Bravely Believe

Brave, Courageous, Gallant, Valiant, Confident!

"When they saw the boldness of Peter and John,
and perceived that they were uneducated and untrained men,
they marveled. And they realized that they had been with Jesus"
(Acts 4:13).

Jesus Christ came to destroy the works of the devil, and then He turned to the church and said, "As the Father sent Me, so send I you!" You have the same assignment to destroy the works of the devil!

Your boldness and confidence will come through your time in union and communion with Jesus Christ.

"If we take up the work of prayer, it will become self-evident that time will be required, so much time that it will become scarcely possible for us to include all our prayer objectives in our prayers every day. We will, therefore, naturally divide them among the six days of the week. And then include them all when Sunday comes, because on that day we have a great deal more time for prayer." O. Hallesby

The most valuable thing that each of us possess is our time. What we give our time to will ultimately define who we are. To be an effective minister will require that you make time alone with God a priority. Confidence and boldness flows from a heart that hears God and loves God. No one else can do this part for you.

What We Give Our Time to Will Ultimately Define Who We Are

Jesus found some men who were willing to give their time to being with Him. It was these followers (not leaders) who Jesus sent out to do the work of the ministry.

"It is impossible to do everything people want you to do. You have just enough time to do God's will. If you can't get it all done, it means you are trying to do more than God intended for you to do (or, possibly, you are watching too much television) . . . It is usually meaningless work, not overwork, which wears us down, saps our strength, and robs our joy." Rick Warren

How to Become Bolder in Your Witness

Praying for boldness is like praying for patience. You will be given opportunities to test out your courage and gain experience. God will call you to a course, and in the midst of that course there will be anxiety and fear. Don't let fear stop you from being bold for God — if you are afraid to step out, do it anyway — step out afraid!

God is ready to pour the weight of His worth into your life! The weight of God's worth brings self-worth. So, invite Him to pour into you. Find people who are bold for Jesus and ask them to pray for you.

Your Decisions Will Determine Your Destiny . . . And the Destiny of Others

Your really can have the kind of bold love that is contagious and brings people around you into an encounter with Jesus, when they encounter you.

I love to be with people who truly believe that entire cities can be saved; people who believe that prayer can change the course of history. It is helpful for me to rub shoulders with individuals who have seen God do miracles and who spur me on. But I cannot rely on other people to fuel my flame. My passion for God and for the world He loves comes through my time of union and communion with Him alone. It is time with God and His Word that turns me into a world-changer. No one else can do this part for me.

If you remember the old Superman television show or the comic books, you will recall how Clark Kent went into a phone booth as a meek and mild news reporter. But then he emerged as a superhero! This is a picture of what happens to us as we meet with God — we are changed into powerful people for His Kingdom!

You might argue that you emerge out of your prayer time the same way you went in (or even frustrated because you didn't feel that you got anywhere). There is a Cross-over point for you.

The Cross-over Point

When I was younger, an older, wiser woman instructed me: "If you want to someday be a woman of prayer, begin TODAY!" I took her at her word and decided that I would begin and get *there* fast. But there is no fast-track for building a strong tower of prayer. You begin at the foundation and build up. (Can you imagine trying to start in the sky to build a tall tower downward?)

The 10,000-Hour Rule

There is research into what is called the "10,000-Hour Rule". This concept is about something that happens when a violinist or a soccer player or a chef put in a lot of hours and gains much experience.

"Psychologists look at the careers of the gifted [and find] innate talent plays a much smaller role than preparations. The thing that distinguishes one performer from another is how hard he or she works. That's it. And what's more, the people at the very top don't work just harder or even much harder than everyone else, they work much, much harder . . . Researchers have settled on what they believe is the magic number for true expertise: ten thousand hours . . . ten thousand hours of practice is required to achieve the level of mastery associated with being a world-class expert — in anything . . . no one has yet found a case in which true world-class expertise was accomplished in less time . . .nor could they find any people who worked harder than everyone else, yet just didn't have what it takes to break the top ranks." Malcolm Gladwell, Outliers, pages 38-41

Of course there are exceptions to this rule as in the case of a child prodigy. But for those of who are average, like me, there is no limit to what can be accomplished if the time is put in.

While researching the 10,000-hour idea, I recalled a story I heard told by Dr. Paul Yonggi Cho. A woman had come to him for healing of a fatal disease. Dr. Cho prayed for the woman but she didn't get well. The woman came again, sicker than ever and asked for more prayer. Given no hope by doctors and sicker than ever, the woman came again. She complained to Dr. Cho that he had not prayed enough. Dr. Cho instructed her to do something herself. He told the woman that when she got desperate enough to write **"By His stripes, I am healed"** (Isaiah 53:5; I Peter 2:24) ten thousand times, she would be healed.

Dr. Cho did not see the woman again for several weeks. But when she did return to see him, she had a doctor's report in her hands. After she had spent so much time writing out the Scripture TEN THOUSAND TIMES, the doctor's report she now carried was one of full cure!

There seems to be something about the 10,000-hour theory and so I decided to do a rough count of how many hours of prayer I had logged in throughout my life. I didn't count the abiding prayer (spontaneously talking to God) that I do throughout each day, nor the prayer in church services or other corporate settings. I simply added up my years of spending at least one hour in "secret" (see Matthew 6:6) daily prayer alone with God. I found that it was around the 10,000-hour mark that I had truly crossed over into a new place with God!

Before the cross-over point, my daily prayer time often felt like work. I would force myself to spend at least one hour a day with God in prayer. This hour would include many aspects of prayer as I would worship God, pray through the Lord's Prayer (Matthew 6:9), pray through my list of people and needs, and try to listen to God. I often wondered if my prayers or time spent in prayer had any effect at all.

But there came a time, an hour when everything FINALLY changed! Prayer became to me as *no longer something I did, but somewhere I went!* Prayer became to me the most wonderful experience of my day, my life and my world! I couldn't wait to get into my prayer closet and shut the door and hear God! The anticipation of my morning prayer time made me want the night to get over with so that morning would come and I could be in the secret place with God again!

I was afraid that the change would be temporary and that I would revert back to prayer being miserable work. But after several years past the cross-over place, I still love my time with God more than any other thing in my life! God speaks to me and I come alive, just as He said, *"It is the Spirit who gives life; the flesh profits nothing. The words that I speak to you are spirit, and they are life"* (John 6:63).

What if I don't hear God in my morning prayer time? I am not frustrated because I know that if I don't hear Him speak right now, I will hear Him in a couple hours or by evening. And there is never a time that I do not hear God speak through the Scripture. I read His Word until I hear Him — even if I have to cancel other plans and appointments.

You may be in the cross-over area, saying, "How long, Lord?" Maybe one day prayer for you is wonderful and the next day you don't even want to pray. And you wonder if you will ever cross over to the place of really abiding in God.

Why Are We Impatient?

Tom and I have visited Moravian Falls, North Carolina, an area where many people have had angelic visitations. This property was once owned by Count von Zinzendorf and the Moravian community of faith, which had been prayed over by the Moravian brethren for over 100 years. People of prayer opened the way for generations that they would not live to see and who would have encounters with God because of their diligent prayer.

Divine order for spiritual dominance is neither impatient nor self-focused. We pray because we care about the generations to come, the desire of God, and to be strengthened in ways that we long for.

The little band of exiles that first left Moravia and settled in North Carolina carried a remarkable prophecy from a man named John Hus. They believed that the *hidden seed* John Hus had spoken of would grow and bear fruit in a hundred-years time . . . "In another century it would finally sprout."

In 1415 John Hus, reformer, father of the Moravians, and extraordinary man of faith was burned at the stake because of his faith. Church officials were convinced that Hus' message would die with him. But his heroic death only fanned into flame his message. Before his death, Hus had prophesied that the message of liberty and spiritual reform would be "a hidden seed" falling into the ground and dying for a season, but one day it would sprout much fruit. And it has.

A prophesy that the hope of revival would not be fulfilled for another hundred years would be very discouraging for us. But the prediction had the opposite effect upon the Moravians. As a people devoted to self-sacrifice, they were honored to be able to help prepare the way for a future generation. They planned with long-term strategy and vision for the future.

I believe that these people of faith would not have blinked at the 10,000-hour theory. I think it might have motivated them that it was so few hours! Let us be like these people of prayer, beginning today by rolling up our sleeves and getting to it!

"Telling to the generation to come the praises of the LORD,
and His strength and His wonderful works that He has done.
For He established a testimony . . . That they may set their hope
in God, and not forget the works of God" (Psalm 78:4-8).

Prayer is Essential to What Happens in the World and in Our Lives

The story of the Prophet Samuel's conception and birth is inspiring as we see the way in which his mother went after God in prayer. Barren and longing for a child, she didn't leave God alone until He answered!

"Hannah was in bitterness of soul, and prayed to the LORD and
wept in anguish. Then she made a vow and said, 'O Lord of Hosts,
if You will indeed look on the affliction of Your maidservant and
remember me, and not forget Your maidservant, but will give
Your maidservant a child" (I Samuel 1:10-11) . . .

If you read the entire story of Hannah's intense intercession, you will find that she abandoned all else to seek God. While other people were satisfied with the temporal, Hannah was consumed with the eternal. Other people were partying and feasting while Hannah fasted. She may have felt very alone.

"Beware of associating with or adopting the attitudes of people, who through their negative outlook and lack of self esteem, will rob you of the greatness God has in store for you." Joel Osteen, Your Best Life Now

God will also call you to a solitary place of retreat where He will birth something new into your life. Throughout history, whenever there was a move of God, it was always accompanied by a concentrated and set-apart time of prayer.

Hannah did not make lightweight or insincere vows to God. She said, "If you will only . . . I will give . . ." and she kept her vow.

If you need breakthrough — if you are barren in spirit — don't be afraid to get on your face before God, and make your vows to Him. God is the One to whom you can pour out your complaints and make your petitions.

Job said, *"My friends scorn me; my eyes pour out tears to God"* (Job 16:20).

King David said, *"I will pour out my complaint before Him; I declare before Him my trouble"* (Psalm 142:2).

Jeremiah said, *"Pour out your heart like water before the face of the Lord. Lift up your hands toward Him for the life of your young children"* (Lamentations 2:19).

Your diligent prayers can change even the spoken word, the prophetic word and the destruction that may already have been set in motion for your life. Consider the story of Hezekiah. A heavy-weight prophet, Isaiah (!) told Hezekiah that he was going to die. But Hezekiah went to God and God heard his prayer and added years to his life! No matter what other people have spoken to you (and no matter how important those people are, whether doctors, parents or prophets); God can intervene on your behalf!

"In those days Hezekiah was sick and near death. And Isaiah the prophet, the son of Amoz, went to him and said to him, 'Thus says the LORD: "Set your house in order, for you shall die, and not live."' Then he turned his face toward the wall, and prayed to the LORD, saying, 'Remember now, O LORD, I pray, how I have walked before You in truth and with a loyal heart, and have done what was good in Your sight.' And Hezekiah wept bitterly. And it happened, before Isaiah had gone out into the middle court, that the word of

the LORD came to him, saying, 'Return and tell Hezekiah the leader of My people, "Thus says the LORD, the God of David your father: 'I have heard your prayer, I have seen your tears; surely I will heal you. On the third day you shall go up to the house of the LORD. And I will add to your days fifteen years'" (II Kings 20:1-6).

Don't leave God alone — prayer will change destinies! Consider what happened with Moses' plea to God for mercy:

"The LORD said to Moses, 'I have seen this people, and indeed it is a stiff-necked people! Now therefore, let Me alone, that My wrath may burn hot against them and I may consume them. And I will make of you a great nation.' Then Moses pleaded with the LORD his God, and said: 'LORD, why does Your wrath burn hot against Your people whom You have brought out of the land of Egypt with great power and with a mighty hand . . . Turn from Your fierce wrath, and relent from this harm to Your people . . .' So the LORD relented from the harm which He said He would do to His people" (Exodus 32:9-14).

God relented because a man asked Him to relent! You can be like Moses and ask God to save your family, your neighbors and your city!

Prayer can actually alter the season for better weather in a time of tribulation! Why else would Jesus have told His disciples to pray for a good season for traveling?

Jesus said, *"Pray that your flight may not be in winter"* (Matthew 24:20).

The power of an intercessor is the most powerful force in the universe. God WILL show Himself strong on your behalf if you will trust Him. Don't settle for less than God has for YOU!

"As a leader or intercessor, God gives us spiritual authority to protect those whom we love. As wide as our range of love, to that degree we have authority in prayer. Such is the unique place we have, whether we are praying for our family, our church, city or nation, people will receive certain victories and protection that they otherwise would not have." Francis Frangipane, <u>America at the Threshold of Destiny</u>, page 36

Will you be bold for God? Will you approach His Throne with boldness and become even bolder?

"Let us therefore come boldly to the throne of grace,
that we may obtain mercy and find grace to help in
time of need" (Hebrews 4:15-16).

As you spend time with God, you will find yourself compelled to help others because of the love you experience with God. Remember, the qualification of Jesus' disciples was *"that they had been with Jesus"* (Acts 4:13). You will find yourself going places and doing things that you never dreamed you could do — all because you forgot about being afraid as you were too busy being focused on Jesus to remember to be scared. I know this for a fact because I live compelled by God's love and astonished at what I can do with His love in me!

God Wants You to Do Miracles for Him

God wants you to ask Him and believe Him for things that are bigger than yourself. He wants to use you to jar the people around you into the reality of His Presence. Wherever Jesus went, there was a continuous supernatural flow of miracles. This very same Jesus resides in you.

Jesus said *"Most assuredly, I say to you, he who*
believes in Me, the works that I do he will do also;
and greater works than these he will do, because I go to
My Father. And whatever you ask in My name, that I
will do, that the Father may be glorified in the Son.
If you ask anything in My name,
I will do it" (John 14:12-13).

The Lord said that you will do greater things. It's time!

Questions

1. When have you confidently stepped out in faith and been amazed at how the Holy Spirit flowed through you?

2. At what times do you feel more confident than others?

3. Do you desire more Holy Spirit power? How will you make more room for the Holy Spirit in your life?

4. What empowered the people of God to speak with boldness according to Acts 4:31?

5. The Apostle Paul asked his friends to pray that he would be bold. Who will you ask to pray for you?

"I thank Christ Jesus our Lord who has enabled me, because He counted me faithful, putting me into the ministry, although I was formerly a . . ." (I Timothy 1:12).

For You to Pray:

Father, make me a bold witness for you! Use my life to bring Your Good News to as many people as I possibly can. Use me to bring Your healing to as many people as You give me. Use me to bring miracles in every situation where a miracle is needed. I give You my hands, my feet, my mouth . . . my life!

"It shall come to pass in that day
That his burden will be taken away from
your shoulder, And his yoke from your neck,
And the yoke will be destroyed because
of the anointing oil" (Isaiah 10:27).

EXTRA TOOLS

I. Anointing Oil Instruction

Understanding:

The practice of anointing with perfumed oil was common among the Hebrews. Anoint describes the procedure of rubbing or smearing a person or thing with oil for the purpose of healing, setting apart and protecting. The anointing oil is symbolic of the joyous presence of the Holy Spirit and is called upon through prayers of faith, while being applied.

Purposes:

<u>Healing</u> — James 5:14

"Is anyone among you sick? Let him call for the elders of the church, and let them pray over him, anointing him with oil in the name of the Lord. And the prayer of faith will save the sick, and the Lord will raise him up. And if he has committed sins, he will be forgiven."

<u>Cleansing</u> — Ruth 3:3

"Therefore wash yourself and anoint yourself."

<u>Protection</u> — Leviticus 8:10

"Moses took the anointing oil, and anointed the tabernacle and all that was in it, and consecrated them."

<u>Consecration, Empowering and Preparation</u> — Exodus 29:7

"You shall put the turban on (Aaron's) head, and put the holy crown on the turban. And you shall take the anointing oil, pour it on his head, and anoint him . . . So you shall consecrate Aaron and his sons."

<u>Strengthening</u> — Isaiah 10:27

"The yoke will be destroyed because of the anointing oil."

<u>Blessing</u> — Hebrews 1:9

"Therefore God, Your God, has anointed You with the oil of gladness more than Your companions."

II. Wisdom in Prayer

Guidelines for Prayer Teams:

Women will pray for women. One woman and one or more men may pray for a man. One man and one or more women may pray for a woman. There will be no one-on-one opposite gender praying.

Before you lay your hands on any person, ask the Holy Spirit. If you are not clear, wait. If you are clear, proceed:

- Ask the individual if you may touch them before putting your hands on them.

- If you are led to touch a person on any area of their body besides the upper back, ask specific permission (this includes the head).

- Men will not lay their hands below the shoulder of a woman.

- Obtain permission from the individual before applying oil. Be ready with memorized Scripture from James 5:14 about this directive.

- Do not offer words of prophecy or advice without an invitation from the individual.

- Ask the person this question, **"What do you want God to do for you?"**

- Listen carefully and tell your own story (if led) very briefly.

- Only pray deliverance for an individual if requested or (in the case of a demonic manifestation) in an urgent situation.

- Do not go into the enemy's camp alone! Partnering in prayer is essential.

- Do not try to impose your will on another person. The only one with completely pure motives and insight is Jesus Christ. Use His Word foremost, not your own:

*"For the word of God is living and powerful,
and sharper than any two-edged sword, piercing even to
the division of soul and spirit, and of joints and marrow,
and is a discerner of the thoughts and intents
of the heart"* (Hebrews 4:12).

**Remember that your prayers are powerful and effective.
Do not take on pressure or burdens that the
Lord Jesus Christ alone carries.**